Awake & Alive to Truth

Finding Truth in the Chaos of a Relativistic World

John L. Cooper

Copyright John L. Cooper, First Printing USA November 2020

This book is dedicated to my mother, Deborah Cooper, who taught me how to play music and about the God who created it. If I close my eyes, I can almost hear her now, cheering me on from that great cloud of witnesses. "Run Johnny! Run! Harder, faster, stronger. There is much gospel work left to do and not much time left to do it."

PRE-SHOW

I REACHED DOWN to pick up my ball, hoping I could squeak out a spare on my second roll. It was after midnight, and I was exhausted after our late-night show. There were only a few more frames, and I could make my way back to the tour bus and pass out from exhaustion.

We were touring as the opening act on a hard rock tour, and the two bands that played after us were extremely successful. And that night, there were a lot of important people in the crowd. King-makers. Gatekeepers. And those people had gathered at this bowling alley with members of the bands.

"Hey John, how's it goin'?"

I looked up, surprised to have my name called by someone that I assumed had no idea who I was. He waved me over to his lane, and I put my ball down and walked over. I suppose my bed would have to wait.

The alley was getting busier by the minute. There were agents, managers, a few famous professional athletes. A couple of record label executives made their way through the crowd. There were radio DJs, playlist programmers. An entourage of women came dressed less for bowling and more for a Maxim shoot.

The guy who had called me over was an agent who booked the show. He introduced me to the promoter and another music business mover and shaker.

"John, no one else is gonna say it, so here it goes. You guys are hot right now and everybody knows it. You've got the songs. You've got the sound. You've got the look...in fact your WHOLE BAND has the look. You've got the show. You've got this uber positivity, and rock radio is starting to look for positivity. Bands are trying to fake it, but you already have it. You've got the personality. You've got this spiritual thing going, and rock fans are starting to crave that, too! This is your moment, and it's time to strike."

Had I heard him right?

It was 2011, before Skillet had sold 12 million albums. Before Monster had 300 million views on YouTube, before we had 4 billion streams worldwide, and prior to touring the world. We had been a band for 14 years and scraped and fought just to pay the bills, and I certainly didn't think any music industry types knew my name. Was this real?

In that moment, all of my dreams came back into focus. All those hours watching music videos as a kid and pretending that I was a rock star. All those hours practicing the piano, practicing the guitar, practicing the bass, practicing my singing, practicing head-banging. The years of my life packing gear and setting up sound systems, playing for a couple of dozen people, shaking hands and taking photos after the show, tearing down all of the gear, and packing it into the trailer just to drive my van all night to the next city. All of it was about to pay off.

"You know what I'm sayin' right, John?" he said, pulling me back into the moment. "It's time to strike…"

I nodded and said something to the effect of "Uhhh, yeah man awesome!" Then he looked at me and put it straight.

"Bro, I'm just gonna say it 'cause you need to hear it. Skillet could be the biggest rock band in the world. But dude, you have to stop talking about Jesus."

Silence.

"Not just talkin' about him…you need to disassociate from your Christian music history. Stop playing Christian shows. Stop doing Christian radio interviews. People just don't take it seriously. The spiritual thing, the positive thing, that's really powerful stuff. But the Jesus stuff hurts your brand. I'm just tellin' you bro."

I listened, thanked him for the encouragement. And I wasn't angry, nor was I conflicted. I realized he actually was doing his best to give me good advice. And truth be told, he was probably right. After all, the industry tends to look at Christian music like the "diet" version of rock music. Fewer calories, but not as good.

He wasn't suggesting I give up my faith, of course. In fact, he explained that if I focused my Christianity on the social aspects of faith rather than on Jesus himself, I actually would be successful on multiple fronts. I would win favor from the rock world. Everyone respects Bono, he said. Simultaneously, I would be showing the love of Christ in action rather than words. Besides, he said, if I were to live my faith without proselytizing, and if we achieved mainstream popularity as a result, wouldn't it bring more attention to my faith in Jesus?

"John," he said as a final argument, "Think of how many poor people you can help in this world if you are rich and famous."

Sometimes lies sound eerily similar to the truth. Sometimes you want something so badly that you cannot trust yourself to even know the difference. Why would God give me these dreams if he did not want me to chase them? Why would he give me this talent?

After the conversation, he invited me to come meet a few of his more famous friends and the girls that were hanging around. I smiled and shook hands and thanked him, but said I needed to get back to the bus. It was late and I was exhausted, and besides, my wife Korey and I had to get up early tomorrow. He smiled, said he looked forward to seeing where Skillet went, and we parted ways.

The next morning, Korey and I talked about it. By noon that day, my decision was made. I could not stop talking about Jesus. I could not stop sharing the truth.

I wonder what my life would be like had I taken his advice. I may have had an even more successful music career. But what would it have cost me? Would I still be married? Would I have raised two young adults who are living for the glory of God? Would I have enjoyed the treasures of the world at the expense of having no treasure in heaven? Even worse, would I have joined the ever-increasing group of ex-Christians who have devolved so far from their faith that it can no longer be recognized as Christianity?

Considering my decision all those years ago, I was reminded of the words of Jesus: "Whoever acknowledges me before men, I also will acknowledge before my father who is in heaven, But whoever denies me before others, I also will deny before my father who is in heaven." (Matt. 10:32-33). In that moment, I decided I would not deny Christ. Nor would I be ashamed of him. Not then. Not ever.

I wrote this book because we are in a time of confusion the likes of which I have never seen. The threads that hold society together are coming unraveled because there is no truth left to bind them. Lies have become truth, truth has become emotion, emotion has become God, God has become whatever one desires—whether rock-and-roll dreams, self-worship, or sexual desire, or whatever. And whatever one desires must be good, right?

Is there a way through this mess? How can we tell the difference between truth and lies when we are constantly bombarded with slippery words which lead us down slippery slopes? Every social media influencer, politician, religious figure, social justice warrior, and every celebrity is vying for your allegiance so they can be more popular, more successful, more powerful. How do you know who to trust?

In my story, I had been offered the promise of fame, fortune, credibility, beautiful women, and star status if I would be willing to compromise my faith in Christ. I chose the unpopular path—"the road less traveled by," as Robert Frost wrote—and that has made all the difference. But that decision was just a continuation of my first decision to trust in God well before my rockstar dreams. It's the night that changed my life. A night I will never forget.

CHAPTER 1:
Built On the Rock

How can I build my life on an unshakeable foundation?

"**There's someone** in my room!" I said it as I wandered into the living room, wearing my Star Wars pajamas and clinging on to my Spider-Man action figure. Her response was firm. My mom didn't play games.

"John, there's no one in your room, now go to bed."

She did not believe me, and why would she? Wasn't this a common five-year old ploy to get out of going to sleep? Hadn't I used other excuses before, like, "I need a drink of water," or "I need to go to the bathroom," or "I lost my Darth Vader toy"?

"Go on," she said again, and I climbed the stairs and crawled under the covers. Peeking out, looking into the darkness of my room, I saw it again, just past my feet. In the shadowed corner of the room, the same figure stood, still staring at my bed. I couldn't see his face, only an outline of a dim shape. What's more, I could feel the presence of the unknown person.

Not knowing if I should fear my father more than the possibility of a stranger in my bedroom, I bolted from my room and ran downstairs for a second time, willing my parents to believe me. "There's someone up there, and he's staring at me!" Short on patience and insisting I was perfectly safe, my father said that if I knew what's good for me, I wouldn't come down a third time. That's when the truth set in. I had to be brave.

I returned to my room, crawled under my covers again. Seconds passed. Then a minute. My eyes adjusted to the dark, and as I looked past my feet, I saw the same figure for a third time. This time was different. I was not afraid. I was surprised. And as I stared down the figure in that corner, words came into my mind. The words were not audible, but they were so real and clear to me that it was just as if my mom or dad had spoken to me face to face. I remember every word, just as if it had happened last night.

You need to give your heart to Jesus.

My first response was childlike and simple. One word.

Okay.

Then in the silence of my bedroom, wondering whether I'd said enough, I added, "Jesus I give my heart to you. You are my boss."

Looking back, it was a natural response. I grew up with a mother who loved Jesus. She read the Bible to me constantly, and I knew the stories of Jesus. I believed God was real. I had heard the phrase, "Give your heart to Jesus," on more than one occasion. But was this vision real?

Some will say I imagined the entire thing, that there was no one there. Admittedly, This wasn't the first time that I thought I saw a person or a thing or a spaceship in my room. I don't presume to be so important that God had to perform a miracle just for me, either. And I don't know if my eyes were playing tricks on me. But truth be told, I do not know nor do I care. My life changed that night, not because of a possible miraculous vision, but rather because of a belief in Jesus that I confessed with my mouth for the first time. No matter what I saw or didn't see, I am sure of this: that night, Jesus became my all. My everything. My rock of truth.

At the time, I had no understanding of the implications of that decision. I didn't realize that in that very moment, alone in my room, the living God was reaching His hand into space and time and pulling me out of darkness. I did not understand that God had softened my heart and gave me the faith that allowed me to believe His words. I certainly had no idea that the John Cooper that had lived for only 5 years on this earth was witnessing the end of his old life and the beginning of a brand new redeemed life. My second birth. I had zero idea of how good, how wonderful, how powerful, and how gracious this God is!

There was a lot I didn't understand, but that moment became the cornerstone of my life—*I gave my heart to Jesus, and He became my boss.* In the years that followed, I'd know Him first as my Savior and my boss. Eventually I'd come to know him as a friend and a father who protects and lovingly disciplines. Eventually, I'd come to a place of total and passionate devotion to the God of the Bible, but it didn't start that way.

During my early teenage years I entered the hardest and loneliest years of my life. My mother—who in many ways had been my spiritual leader—had lost her three-year battle with cancer. I was fourteen-years old, hurt, confused, and incredibly lonely. During that time, I prayed and prayed to God, my Savior and my boss. But the

> **Then in the silence of my bedroom, wondering whether I'd said enough, I added, "Jesus I give my heart to you. You are my boss."**

loneliness would not go away. The hurt was not healed. Nothing helped. All that I heard was silence. But one night something changed.

I don't recall how the notion popped in to my head. Perhaps, I read it in my Bible. Maybe someone read it to me. Whatever the case, in the quiet of my room, I asked Jesus if I could know Him in a different way, praying, "Jesus, you are my boss. You are my Savior. But would it be alright if I could know you as a friend?" The moment I prayed it, I felt His response. (I know no other way to say this.) God placed this truth from the Bible in my heart and head. It was as if He was saying, "Yes, but I won't just come to you now as a friend, but also as a dad."

In that moment, tears of joy and pain ran down my face. In fact, I'd never cried so hard as I did that night. Alone in the dark on my bed in Memphis, Tennessee, the God of the entire universe reached into my life and called me by name. I don't know what else was happening at midnight on the streets of Memphis, but one thing was certain. The kingdom of God was silently going about the business of shattering the kingdom of darkness and rescuing me, the broken hearted. It was the night I learned that God is a faithful friend.

These two moments have been foundational in my life, and everything else has been built upon them. God is my Father and Jesus is my Lord. I have come to believe the words Paul wrote to the church in Corinth, "yet for us there is one God, the Father, from whom are all things and for whom we exist, and one Lord, Jesus Christ, through whom are all things and through whom we exist" (1 Corinthians 8:6).

Jesus is also my Savior. I stand on the words of the apostle Peter, who wrote, "But grow in the grace and knowledge of our Lord and Savior Jesus Christ. To him be the glory both now and to the day of eternity. Amen" (2 Peter 3:18) .

But Jesus is not just my Lord and Savior. He is also my friend. He intimated as much when he said,

> Greater love has no one than this, that someone lay down

his life for his friends. You are my friends if you do what I command you. No longer do I call you servants, for the servant does not know what his master is doing; but I have called you friends, for all that I have heard from my Father I have made known to you. (John 15:13-15 ESV)

The older I get, the more I realize the words of God are true! They are life! And the more I understand Him, the more I come to know Him, the more wonderful He's grown in my eyes.

This is my story of becoming awake and alive to truth. Not a version of truth. Not partial truth. Not cultural axioms of truth. Not what I *feel* is true. I became alive to the eternal Truth. Truth that never changes, one that lies at the end of the pursuit for meaning. In a time when so many are falling into destruction, this truth has kept me safe, and it will keep me safe for the rest of my life and in the eternal life to come.

Jesus the Rock of Truth

Knowing the mantra of the rock-and-roll industry is "sex, drugs, and rock n roll," people often ask me how I've managed to keep my faith strong in today's entertainment world. How have I avoided immorality and the self-worship of the modern celebrity influencer? How have I raised kids who know where to find truth in a society that is opposed to God?

The answers to these questions—and every other question of human existence—are found in a simple question. In fact, it began with the question I first explored as a child: *What does it mean to say that God is the boss?* When I called God "my boss," it was my five-year-old way of calling Him Lord. It was my way of saying I would trust and obey whatever He says. Even when I don't understand, even when I don't want to, I will try and obey because He is the boss. He is in control. He is Lord. And I still take that approach today.

The psalmist wrote, "Our God is in the heavens; he does all that he pleases" (Psalm 115:3). That sums it up! He is Lord and does whatever He pleases. Whatever he does is *right*. As a result, I have to live by His Word and do what He says. When I don't, I have to change my ways.

As I grew older my understanding of repentance deepened. But even as a 5 year old I understood that I had disobeyed "the boss" many times. Like when I had fist fights with my older brother-or when my friend next door and I broke all of the seats in his swing set and then lied about it to our parents. I understood that I needed to ask forgiveness for these wrongs, and that I needed to do what the boss commanded going forward. Still, it wasn't always easy. I haven't always loved it! And can I be honest? There were many times I chose my own path instead of God's because in the moment I thought that I would prefer it. In those moments, sin seemed fun until I realized I had hurt both myself and the people I love. Every time I don't follow the boss, I find myself a slave to the very things that cause me pain and suffering.

But there is good news. There's a way to end this cycle of pain and self-destruction!

The Profit of Following the Truth

In high school athletics, our trainer led us in stretches prior to working out. I hated those stretches and didn't believe it helped. It was uncomfortable, boring, and seemed unnecessary. But the older I get, the more I realize that stretching is for my benefit. It protects me from injury, enhances my workout, helps my recovery, and it keeps me limber. And what's true of stretching is true of obeying God's Word. If you do it—even when it seems boring or uncomfortable—you'll be stronger, happier, and more fulfilled.

I wish that I could convince everyone of the profitability of obeying God's Word. In this book, that's what I'll attempt to do. Here, I'll write in depth about how to find and apply truth. But before we do, we'll start with the foundation, with the understanding that God calls us to obey Him and the truth He's given us through Jesus. Whatever Jesus says is unquestionably right, and if it were not, then following Him is a waste of time.

Jesus didn't come preaching an easy message, but it was a message that contained a great promise. He said:

> Everyone then who hears these words of mine and does them will be like a wise man who built his house on the rock. And the rain fell, and the floods came, and the winds blew and beat on that house, but it did not fall,

> because it had been founded on the rock. And everyone who hears these words of mine and does not do them will be like a foolish man who built his house on the sand. And the rain fell, and the floods came, and the winds blew and beat against that house, and it fell, and great was the fall of it. **(Matt. 7:24-27)**

Jesus knew the truth. Life is hard. Storms will come. Do you want to be someone whose life stands in the midst of those storms? Would you like to be someone who has a foundation so strong that you can weather whatever life throws at you, no matter how hard the trial or how hurtful the pain? When others wallow in misery, do you want joy? Then pay attention to Jesus, and build your life on the rock of His truth. If you do, you will have hope where others have fear. You can rest assured that you are destined for glory when others suffer from dissatisfaction of a destiny unfulfilled.

But before we get ahead of ourselves, know this: We must be prepared to obey Him when it's difficult, uncomfortable, and when we do not understand. And this leads me to something often overlooked in this passage of Scripture. Hearing and believing the truth is not enough. Look at the verse directly before it:

> Not everyone who says to me, 'Lord Lord,' will enter the Kingdom of heaven, but the one who does the will of my Father who is in heaven. On that day many will say to me, 'Lord, Lord, did we not prophecy in your name, and cast out demons in your name, and do many mighty works in your name?' And then will I declare to them, 'I never knew you; depart from me, you workers of lawlessness'. **(Matt 7:21-23)**

The one who hears, claims belief, yet does not act according to His words is precisely the kind of person Jesus "never knew." These are the people who have built their house on the sand, and when the storms come, they will not stand strong.

Matthew Henry, the seventeenth century English minister and author, wrote concerning this passage:

> All the sayings of Christ, not only the laws he has enacted, but the truths he has revealed, must be done by us. They're a light, not only to our eyes, but to our feet, and are designed not only to inform our judgements, but to reform our hearts and lives: nor do we indeed believe them, if we do not live up to them. Observe, it is not enough to hear Christ's sayings, and understand them, hear them, and remember them, hear them and talk of them, repeat them, dispute for them, but we must hear and do them.[1]

As Henry well knew, building upon the rock of God's Word is not just about hearing or believing the the right things. Rather, building a life on Christ means acting on the Word of God.

It must be noted, of course, that this Scripture does not mean that salvation is dependent upon us perfectly obeying God's Word. That's impossible! No one has managed that since the dawn of mankind. That said, simply acknowledging Jesus's truth is not the same as trusting in Jesus. In fact, for many, believing Jesus's words without acting on them often leads to more frustration and confusion. What do I mean?

Consider the businessman who knows Jesus's teachings about integrity, but shades the truth to increase profits. Will he ultimately be satisfied with his wealth?

Consider the porn addict who knows Jesus's commands about lust, but cannot seem to quit. Isn't he followed by shame?

Consider the pastor or influencer who claims to follow Jesus when its convenient or beneficial, but refuses to follow Him when it is unpopular. Doesn't she second-guess herself?

All of us have sinned, so I use these examples not to cast stones at others, but rather to bring freedom! When you know the truth of God's Word but do not follow through, that truth becomes a source of judgment. This is why so many self-professed followers of Jesus have become disillusioned. Some have become utterly miserable. Again, Matthew Henry says,

> ...if our hearing be not the means of our obedience, it

will be the aggravation of our disobedience. Those who only hear Christ's sayings, and do them not, sit down in the midway to heaven, and that will never bring them to their journeys end. They are akin to Christ only by the half-blood, and our law allows not such to inherit.[2]

If we actually believe God, then we will trust His Word. If we believe He has the answers, that He is always right, that He is always loving, we'll do what he says. But is is such a thing possible? Really?

TRUSTING THE TRUTH IN LIFE, DEATH, AND EVERYTHING IN BETWEEN

Death is a difficult thing to handle at any age. There are no easy answers and no quick fixes. Truth is, most people in my life would have understood if I had become angry or blamed God after the death of my mother. It would be natural to ask how a good God could allow my mom to die, especially at such a young age. And though I knew the Bible says ".that for those who love God all things work together for good, for those who are called according to his purpose" (Romans 8:28), I recall asking myself, "how is this possibly working for my good?"

Thankfully, my mom prepared me for the worst. She believed she would be healed, but she often said, "If God doesn't heal me, you cannot and must not be mad at God. He is always good, and He is always in control." And after her passing, though I didn't understand, I took her advice. I chose to believe in God's goodness rather than blame Him.

Still, I didn't hide from my emotions. I told God that I didn't understand why He'd allowed her death. I told Him I was confused and brokenhearted. But even as I poured my heart out in prayer, I told him I'd still act upon His Word and trust Him. And as I did, God always showed up. Big time! He comforted me. He loved me. He led me. In the words of a killer band,

> If you can calm the raging seas
> You can calm the storm in me
> You're never too far away
> You never show up too late[3]

The Psalmist said it much better: "God is our refuge and strength, a very present help in trouble" (Psalm 46:1). I learned this from the youngest age. Even though I wish my mom hadn't died, I've come to learn that this life is not about my wishes and my desires, but rather it is about God's will and His ultimate glory. Spending a life surrendered to the glory of God brings salvation, peace, meaning, and soul-satisfaction.

Through this book, I'm inviting you on a journey. I'm inviting you to know and understand a God who loves you. In fact, He loves you so much that He won't allow you to have peace while you continue chasing your own pleasures, your own desires, or your own ego because those paths lead to death. I'm inviting you to explore a truth that answers the hardest human questions, including the questions of life and death. I'm inviting you to explore a truth that's eternal and unchanging, one that will bring you unimaginable fulfillment. Follow me into this journey. Come and see the marks of a life built on truth. Then turn and build your life on the Rock.

CHAPTER 2:
Your Truth My Truth the Truth

Why does truth seem to change everyday?

"Where were you yesterday, dude? You totally missed band practice."
Band practice? I completely forgot.

I was in tenth grade, and it was only seven months after my mother's death. I played in the marching band at school, and we'd had an after school rehearsal that more than slipped my mind. In fact, it didn't even ring a bell. I was not a great student, but I wasn't the worst either. I certainly wasn't a troublemaker and did my best to honor my commitments. I would never have intentionally skipped band practice. I knew I was dead-meat.

After class that day, my band director called me into his office, and I was ready. When he asked me why I missed, I did what any self-respecting teenager would do. I lied. "My best friend had just turned 16," I said, "and we always promised that the first thing we were going to do when he got his license was drive out to my mother's grave."

That's right. I did it. I used my mother's death as a cheap excuse to get out of trouble. Even as I write this, those old emotions wash over me. Shame seems to have a kind of immortality. It's like Jason Voorhees, the killer from the 1980's cult classic film series "Friday the 13th." Just when you think he's dead, he comes back to haunt you (#shamelivesagain).

The band director liked me. He knew my mother before she died, and he liked her, too. Had I just told him the truth, that I'd forgotten, he probably would have believed me. Had I said that I wasn't feeling like myself, that I was struggling in my personal life, he probably would have empathized with me. Instead, though, I lied because I convinced myself that I had a "greater truth."

A greater truth?

That's right.

Use some imagination. Put yourself in my shoes, and I think you'll see where I was coming from. My mother had died. I was depressed. I was lonely. I was angry. Nobody on earth knew what I was going through or how I felt. I didn't understand why God would let this happen. I probably needed a therapist. Besides, I honestly had not skipped on purpose. Therefore, the greater truth was the one I *felt*, the one that would get me out of trouble.

Maybe you can empathize with my feelings. Maybe you can excuse my behavior because I really was going through a tough time. However, in regards to what is true, feelings and empathy are irrelevant. The truth is that I missed rehearsal and then lied about it. Period. End of story. It's the only truth in the equation. And its ugly.

THE VERSIONS OF TRUTH

In 2018, we watched history unfold during the Brett Kavanaugh Senate confirmation hearings. Kavanaugh was up for a seat on the United States Supreme Court when Christine Blasey Ford made an earth shattering sexual assault allegation against him. It allegedly occurred 26 years prior, and the accuser did not recall the date it happened, much less the year. She claimed the assault took place at a party with other people, though none of them recall it happening. And perhaps the assault happened; perhaps it didn't. For purposes of this discussion, it's actually irrelevant. What is relevant is that it was the first time I watched national leaders state we must believe "her truth."

Her truth.

I recall wondering why they were using such odd language. Before that moment, I'd not realized the implications of language like "her truth" or "his truth" or "my truth." I just thought that I was getting old and didn't understand "young people" talk. Wrong.

The insinuation being made was that whether or not the assault literally happened, Blasey Ford's truth is a higher truth. Rather than appealing to facts, evidence, or a trial, her truth appeals to a greater sense of how women have historically been mistreated. So, as a woman who is inherently a victim of the patriarchy and secondly, as an alleged victim of sexual abuse, she has access to a higher level of truth than a man.

Still not following?

It goes something like this: Women have been assaulted, harassed, and paid poorly in the workplace for generations. The men who have assaulted and harassed them have gotten away with it. Therefore, what she "feels" is paramount and justifies her claim to truth, just as I was justified in lying to my band director. It may not be literally true, but it "feels" true, particularly when memories are hazy.

This book is not political, and I'm sure some of you reading this book believe him, and some believe her. But this example illustrates how our ideas of truth have shifted in drastic ways over the last ten years. Ten years ago society would have generally believed that discovering the truth of what happened 26 years ago would be impossible. And this does not mean there are possible versions of truth regarding the alleged sexual abuse. There is an answer—he either did it or he didn't—but unfortunately, we may never find out.

The Brett Kavanugh confirmation is a symptom of a greater problem, and this is not just harping on semantics. There is a greatly confusing rhetoric rising up in our culture that is a result of a melting pot of various philosophies. This rhetoric comes from post-modernism, relativism, marxism, atheism, the new age movement (which is nothing more than an updated form of ancient gnosticism), and even culture movements like the push for diversity and inclusion, the social justice movement, and critical race theory. The language used by these various philosophies is loaded with academic meaning and insinuations that often go overlooked due to how ubiquitous these philosophies are. The result? We are witnessing a complete shift of worldview and paradigm right before our eyes. Not only in America, but on a global scale.

The fact that the rhetoric has become on trend in pop-culture has somewhat disguised the underpinnings of this new dominant philosophical empire. For instance, only two decades ago it would not be shocking or even surprising to hear that Jesus is *the* Truth. You wouldn't have heard that Jesus is "my truth" or "your truth" or "a version of truth." But claiming Jesus is THE TRUTH today is often deemed bigoted and intolerant.

Also interesting, 20 years ago even those who disbelieve in Christianity wouldn't have claimed to have their "own version" of truth. They would disbelieve in the God of the Bible while holding a differing truth claim. In other words, society has altogether moved away from a belief in absolute objective truth. As we will see, this has led to chaos in the world and

> *The true follower of Jesus believes that Jesus is the one and only truth. And if this sounds exclusive, that's because it is!*

even within the church. So much so that there are even modern Christians who believe in versions of truth. Or at the least, they believe that God's Word is fairly malleable. This is a tragedy and a fallacy. The true follower of Jesus believes that Jesus is the one and only truth. And if this sounds exclusive, that's because it is!

How have we gotten to this place of relative truth? Let's turn to some of the ruling philosophies of our culture and see.

Philosophy #1: Post-modernism

We are living in a time that can best be described as philosophical stew. A little bit of this, a little dash off that. One of the biggest driving influences of our society has been the philosophy of post-modernism. Post modernism is difficult to comprehend, but Brian Duigan defines it as "a late 20th century movement characterized by broad skepticism, subjectivism, or relativism; a general suspicion of reason; and an acute sensitivity to the role of ideology in asserting and maintaining political and economic power."[4]

Post modernists do not believe in objective truth, nor do they believe that something can be objectively false. To simplify, post modernists believe that there is no such thing as absolute truth. They also believe that reality is nothing more than a conceptual construct. Post modernists reject absolute moral values. Therefore there can be nothing that is absolutely good and nothing that can be absolutely bad.

No absolute truth, no absolute morality, no absolute reality—it's a convenient nightmare.

Philosophy #2: Relativism

A somewhat similar philosophy that is an off-shoot of post modernism is called relativism. The Oxford Dictionary defines relativism as: the doctrine that knowledge, truth, and morality exist in relation to culture, society, or historical context, and are not absolute.[5] In other words, relativism is *almost* synonymous with post modernism, though they are slightly different in one aspect. Post modernism says there is no truth. Relativism says that while there is no absolute truth, there are differing versions of truth depending on culture and historical context. In other words, truth is not absolute, but it can be *true for now* or *more true* than something else.

According to the Stanford Encyclopedia of Philosophy,

> Relativism has been, in its various guises, both one of the most popular and most reviled philosophical doctrines of our time. Defenders see it as a harbinger of tolerance and the only ethical and epistemic stance worthy of the open-minded and tolerant. Detractors dismiss it for its alleged incoherence and uncritical intellectual permissiveness.[6]

I suppose you can count me among the detractors.

In a relativistic society, an obvious question arises: who decides what is true for what period of time and in what culture? And this, I think, is the crux of much of our dilemma as a society. There are no rules, no absolutes, no guides. The people fight over what is true, and often, facts don't matter.

Do you agree that people seem more divided today than ten years ago? 20 years ago? In an era of tolerance and self-proclaimed love, why are we getting angrier at one another? One big reason is because we no longer have common ground in the truth. One side proclaims Kavanaugh innocent, the other guilty. One side says God is good, the other says God is a construct created to control people. If the truth is relative, there is nothing to keep people from moving to the extremes.

It should go without saying that when a society shares the truth, when they have a common moral framework and shared goals, it will be more united. But in a society that does not believe in absolute truth or morality, it will not take long for one person's desire to clash against another's. Sound familiar?

Unbeknownst to many of us, the philosophies of relativism and post modernism have become the bedrock of modern culture's view on truth. And it happened very, very quickly.

The Ugly Stepchildren of Postmodern Thought

This isn't about politics, but the applications to politics are inescapable. (You may have noticed?) Have you wondered why politics has become so divisive? Partially, It's the fruit of postmodernism. Duignan writes,

> In the 1980's and '90's, academic advocates on behalf of various ethnic, cultural, racial, and religious groups embraced postmodern critiques of contemporary Western society, and postmodernism became the unofficial philosophy of the new movement of 'identity politics.'[7]

If you don't know, identity politics is a system in which everyone in society is broken up into identity groups based on race, gender, economic status, and sexual orientation. Politically, these identity groups are all influenced to think and vote monolithically. But it is not only about political power such as voting. It is also about obtaining an asserting influence in general.

Identity politics so often drives academia, beginning at pre-school and comes to full fruition in the university. It is also used by the media and by social media to influence outcomes. And if identity politics is the step-child of postmodernism, then it is fair to say that it gave birth to a generation of what we now call social justice warriors, people who wage war against the society on behalf of various identity groups.

Postmodernism and the Rise of Marxism

We cannot forget the ever increasing power of Marxism. Admittedly, Post modernism and Marxism are quite different. However, once you understand how a little Marxism has crept into the postmodern stew of the day, the things you watch on the news everyday begin to make more sense.

Jordan Peterson states that because postmodernism claims there are innumerable truths and therefore innumerable ways to perceive the same outcome, it is impossible to interpret events properly. He then says, "That's the fundamental claim. An immediate secondary claim (and this is where the Marxism emerges) is something like 'since no canonical manner of interpretation can be reliably derived, all interpretation variants are best interpreted as the struggle for power.'"[8]

This is where the influence of Marxism is clear. According to Peterson, postmodernists disbelieve in absolute reality. Therefore, how can we all experience a version of reality together? Put another way, whose reality wins? Is it the rich person's reality or the poor person's reality? The man's reality or the woman's realty? If everything in the universe is based on the struggle for power, then our perceived reality is determined by the powerful. In this mode of thinking, truth (subjective, relative truth) is determined by those who rule. The Marxists influence in post modernism aims to heighten the voice of the minority (the oppressed) and silence the voice of the majority (the oppressors) to achieve cultural revolution. Who are the oppressed? Every identity group that is not white, male, straight, cisgendered, and Christian. If the powerless can achieve revolution, then they can literally change truth and reality. Yes, you heard me—change truth. Change reality. This is partly how identity politics emerged and why it has become so powerful.

The natural result of all of this is the rise of "intersectionality." Intersectionality claims that the identity groups that have long held power have a certain kind of privilege. The marginalized groups and the disadvantaged are the victims of the privileged. As a result, those who ascribe to an intersectional view believe society has collectively and unjustly interpreted reality through the lens of the privileged and the powerful.

Furthermore, those who ascribe to this philosophy contend that the power structure needs to be turned upside down. In this new system, the male, white, straight, and wealthy person should now be at the bottom of the food chain. The female, person of color, queer, or transgender person should be at the top. For each step you climb higher on the victimhood ladder, your truth is deemed more true. The female has "secret truth" that a male cannot. The person of color has "secret truth" that a white person cannot. If combined, the female person of color gets double points. Therefore, the obvious conclusion is that the more you have been victimized or marginalized, the higher your consciousness is to secret truth. (The technical term for this "secret truth" is "standpoint epistemology," and it has already made major inroads into most formerly conservative denominational structures and seminaries).

Relativism in the Church

This may all seem like a major departure from the question at hand concerning the truth of Christ, but it is not. First, it is relevant to the issues of secular society and the house built upon the sand that I discussed in Chapter One. Can you see why life has become so chaotic? If morality shifts everyday, how can anyone live a virtuous life? The marginalized are all at war with each other, trying to decide day by day who is the most victimized in order to see who is the most powerful. Whoever is left standing at the end of the day can burn down any tradition that one perceives as privileged. And if you follow the logic, anything and everything in history that was built and has lasted must have been built by the powerful, proven by the fact that it still exists. Therefore, it must be torn down! This includes our views on Christianity, The Church, The Bible, the family, raising children, everything.

Does that sound extreme? Let me ask you, when is the last time you heard someone say that they are leaving the Christian faith because Christians don't care enough about social justice? Or women's rights? Or environmentalism? My guess is that you've heard it in the last month. Why would anyone turn their back on the life changing truth of Christ, simply due to a lack of social justice emphasis by their local Church? The answer is found in these powerfully influential philosophies of our day. The historically powerful (Christianity in this instance) must be stripped of virtue due to the hierarchy of victimhood. The only way to regain virtue is to bow your knee to the higher truth of the victimized. Many who have walked away from Christianity altogether would rather be rewarded with perceived virtue from a relativistic world than receive the gift of righteousness from an absolutely Holy God.

But this sort of cultural relativism isn't the most alarming thing. Most alarming is how quickly many in the church have adopted the relativistic thoughts of the day. Shockingly, many Christians are beginning to interpret morality as being subjective! If the Bible is clear about an issue concerning sexual morality, and if we don't prefer what the Bible says, we just simply appeal to a "higher truth." (As if a higher truth than God's Word could even possibly exist!) I cannot think of any better example for building a house upon the sand than this sort of thinking.

Imagine being in a relationship with a spouse that doesn't believe in absolute truth. "Have you been seeing other men, honey?" She says she has not, but in reality she has, and she feels quite justified in doing it. "He doesn't listen to me," she says. "He doesn't respect me, makes all of the decisions, and on top of it all he's got a gut." She has adopted a "higher truth." She has made herself the victim, so the truth is what she says it is, particularly if it robs him of power.

If relativism were the only result, it'd be bad enough. But it's not. Along with relativism, a sort of anti-authority sentiment has crept in. If historically, preachers have power, then why should I listen to them? What's worse, many preachers no longer teach with any sort of conviction because they fear they will offend or lose members from their congregations. Capitulating to the culture, they undercut the authority of Scripture and fail to teach the orthodox doctrine of the Christian faith taught by Christian leaders for centuries. Does this sound too conspiratorial? Too harsh? Whenever I hear or read a historically held Bible truth, it is always followed by angry self-professing Christians who are offended by it. Any teaching on repentance, the holiness of God, judgement, or sexual morality will be sure to invoke a chorus of people saying, "That's not the Jesus I know!" I've heard it so often that I have come to agree with them. That's right—the Jesus of the Bible is not the Jesus they know.

BURNING DOWN TRADITION, BURNING DOWN SOCIETY

Society wants to burn down tradition, and many Christians are going right along with it. Some Christians are starting to believe that in order to teach some truths, you must first have suffered an evil or been a victim of some sort. For instance, the only person who can guide someone who is suffering from self harm is someone who has also suffered from self harm. Or perhaps only people with mental health issues can preach truth to those with mental health issues. It has become quite en vogue in the Church to believe that the only prerequisite to preaching truth to the struggling is to have had your life fall apart in some way. This is, of course, nonsense. Otherwise, our sinless savior, Jesus Christ, could not have been called "wonderful counselor." I would argue, therefore, that it is not our former bondage to sin or our identities that makes us adequate to preach truth. It is the Spirit of God alone that equips us with an understanding of Scripture and the anointing to speak truth to the hurting.

Truth is revealed by God and God alone. The identity you belong to—the color of your skin, your gender, or your economic status—cannot be a prerequisite for understanding the truth. Whether you are proletariat or bourgeois (as Marx taught) or whether you are privileged or oppressed will not grant anyone access. Truth, virtue, and righteousness are defined by God and God alone. And that's why we must turn our focus back to Jesus, God in the flesh. The living Truth.

JESUS IS THE TRUTH. THE TRUTH IS IN JESUS

For the Christian, relativism is not an option. The very nature of the philosophy calls in to question every possible aspect of God's existence. What's more, it calls our own existence into question. (If everything is relative, can you be sure that your existence is real, that it's not just a dream or a computer simulation or the imagination of some alien race?) So, why are so many Christians afraid to vocalize the exclusivity of truth? Going back to our example of a cheating spouse, would any husband or wife accept a relativist viewpoint in the truth of their marriage? Of course not!

> *For the Christian, relativism is not an option.*

Jesus said, "I am the way, and the truth, and the life. No one comes to the Father except through me." (John 14:6) And directly after Jesus says that he is the truth, Phillip asked Jesus to "show us the Father." He was referring to God the Father, who is the first person of the Trinity. Jesus answered with an incredible statement proving he is one with God the Father." Do you not believe that I am in the Father and the Father is in me? The words that I say to you I do not speak on my own authority, but the Father who dwells in me does his works." (John 14:10)

In these words, Jesus claimed to be *the* Truth. He claimed that he and God are one, inseparable in power and deity. In other words, Jesus claimed to be God.

There are many who appreciate the ethical life and words of Jesus, but do not believe that Jesus is the Savior of the world. Let it be stated clearly that to be a true follower of Jesus one must believe that he is the truth and that he is who he said he is—God in the flesh. It is not enough to believe he was a good moral teacher.

If Jesus is indeed who he says he is, he is God and cannot lie. (Believing in a god who goes around lying and making outrageous claims is ludicrous.) What's more, if he claimed to be God and was not, he cannot be considered a great man, because he was a liar. This is why I am continually baffled at those who claim Jesus was a great man yet do not believe his words.

To make it practical, if you had a friend named Ralph who helps the poor and the orphans, but who claimed to be God, would you call him a good man and moral teacher? Would you keep hanging out with him without begging him to seek professional counseling for his God complex?

Where Do We Go From Here?

As we wrestle against the effects of relativism, let us think briefly about the absurdity of it all. No one actually believes postmodern thought. Sure, I realize many claim that they believe in it, but practically speaking, how many of them disbelieve that we are living in reality? That the sky is not real, but rather perceived? That they are living in the Matrix? As Morpheus said to Neo, "You think that's air you're breathing?" To believe in a physical, tangible world requires more than believing in your truth. It means believing in some absolute truth.

I tested the waters of relativism when I lied to my band director all those years ago. I'm not going to lie, the water was warm. It was nice for a while. But a wonderful fiction is fiction none the less. And that fiction led me to so much guilt and shame. And the sooner I jettisoned that philosophy, the better off I was and the easier it was to live in the knowledge of absolute truth.

If you're willing to accept the absolute truth that Jesus is more than a good and ethical man, but is in fact God, then it is time for us to venture onwards. How can we learn about absolute truth, and how does it impact our lives? Let's turn to the Scriptures, where we find the truth about the Way, the Truth, and the Life.

CHAPTER 3:

In the Name of God

How can I know that truth never changes?

"$A^2 + B^2 = C^2$" the teacher said.

How can there be letters in math? I was completely baffled. Most things math-adjacent baffle me honestly. Math is God's punishment.

"John, The letters represent..."

That is all I heard, because I just stopped listening. I objected on principle, needing some proof that the letters *actually* represented the sides of a triangle. What's more, how could we know this equation would always be true? Further still, why should I care about triangles or squares and how would I possibly use this in the future? On top of it all, I could barely even pronounce the word "hypotenuse," much less identify it on any given triangle.

The teacher was unrelenting.

"John, did you hear me?"

"How do we know this formula actually works?" I asked.

"Just memorize it, John!" she said, before adding, "It doesn't matter whether you understand where it came from, it is simply true. Just accept it and move on."

I did not accept it, and consequently, I struggled to pass the test. But despite my stubbornness, there are men and women from all races, ethnicities, nationalities, and socioeconomic classes who are successful in mathematics because they all agree on one thing: the truths of mathematics are absolute. They've accepted it.

Any mathematician's career must be built on the truth of mathematical formulas. In fact, there are are always foundational truths that form the basis of every discipline. And if we're going to succeed in those disciplines, assent to those fundamental truths is required.

The same is true for building a life. There are fundamental truths that will make our lives infinitely more enjoyable and ultimately more satisfying. What are those rules?

The Scriptures teach that a wise man builds his life on the rock of Christ.

Building on his teachings, we can withstand the rains and the winds of life, at least, that's his claim. It's a claim that makes sense, too. After all, if you wouldn't set foot in a building built by someone who treats the laws of mathematics and general construction principles as subjective, why should you treat the building of your life any differently.

But that begs the question: Are there any absolute truths for life? There are! We have a proven set of guiding principles in the Scriptures. But wait. The Scriptures provide more than just a set of guiding principles. They provide the very promises of God! But we must ask, how can we know if His promises are true?

The Bible is often called "The Word of God." What else could be more absolute than God's words? Would a rational person put their opinions on one side of a scale and weigh it against God's words? Science on one side of the scale against God's words? If God is real, then His words must be absolute. He can have no equal. He can not be outweighed. To believe in God but not trust His words would be madness. This is why Christians believe in *the authority of Scripture*. Scripture is the final word. It is the wisest of all wisdom. It is the unshakeable foundation. Everything in the galaxies, from the deepest expanse of the cosmos to the smallest microscopic atom and everything in the seen and unseen realms bow down to the authority and supremacy of God. He is the author of life, the creator of the world. He created everything by the *word* of His power. And as we will see, His word is also His authority, and His word is Him.

The Foolishness of God's Word

The Bible says a lot about God's Word, but first, we must confront a simple fact. The Bible will always be foolishness to those who do not come to the Scriptures with a changed heart and mind. Throughout the Bible, they see contradiction. They read about miracles and impossible acts and consider them as fables or fairy tales.

The one who hears God's words with faith is like a blind man who has just been healed and opened his eyes for the very first time! God's words are illuminating, and through it, you can see the true shape, color, and context of the world. And once you see the truth of God's word, you cannot help but to see God's truth everywhere and in everything!

To make the point, let's start with a more foundational principle. If God exists, then He certainly must be infinite. Not only does this make sense, but it is is agreeable to philosophers and theologians from all sorts of vantage points—those from Christian and Jewish heritages, as well as those in the platonic and socratic traditions.

If this is true, though, how can we expect to fully understand an infinite mind when we are so very limited? Should we read the Bible and think it absurd because we cannot fully understand it? Not many (if any) humans alive today have the natural wisdom and logic of Plato, yet we watch a handful of Ted Talks about Christianity and then chastise God's words because they are a mystery to finite minds. Are there complexities? Mysteries? Unexplainable supernatural events in the Bible? Well I would hope so, or else this infinite God doesn't seem all that different to me than finite humans. And if the Bible was full of only explainable events, do you think people would say, "Because the bible is full of explainable events, I Absolutely believe it!" Somehow I doubt it.

There are those who claim the Bible is foolishness because the eye-witness accounts of Jesus differ. But this argument doesn't hold up even in our own real world contexts.

What do I mean?

Imagine you went to a concert with a group of your friends. Afterwards you asked each of them to tell you about the show. One indicates the singer opened the concert wearing a leather jacket while pyrotechnics went off in the background. Another says that the singer wore a sleeveless shirt and body surfed through the crowd. Would these things necessarily be contradictions? Which friend is lying? Who do you trust? But isn't the answer is obvious? At one point the singer wore a leather jacket and there were pyrotechnics , and at another point he took off his jacket and crowd surfed. Your two friends aren't lying to you. They each focused on different events and were impacted by the same events and words in different ways.

To the heart that approaches the gospels of Jesus with faith, this is extremely obvious. To those without faith, though, these represent foolish contradictions.

Another objection often voiced is that even if God's original words were true, they were recorded by human hands, and therefore were prone to human error.

Sadly, this theory is gaining ground even within the Church. I hear congregants asking, "Can a sovereign God really trust that humans won't mess up His words?" Again, if we start from the premise that there is an infinite God, then we must conclude that God understood this possibility. Still, He trusted the power and sovereignty of His words to people. (This book does not tackle the issue of inherency of Scripture in detail. If you are looking for a great resource on that check out Dr. James White's book *Scripture Alone*.)

But even those who turn to the Scriptures with a certain amount of faith still wrestle with the authority of Scripture. Some Christians put their trust in Christ, yet they believe that the Bible is nothing more than a guide. This is error of the gravest kind. To them, the Bible is not absolute authority, nor is it meant to be taken literally.

There are other Christians who take a higher view, who describe it as "God's advice to us". Sort of like if God had a diary and He wrote down thoughts and axioms. Something like, "Love your neighbor, help the poor, be a good person, and never wear white after Labor Day." These Christians weigh God's Word as principles that are more true than any other principles. This approach still falls short of the power of God's Word.

Moving even higher on the ladder of the importance of Scripture would be the Christian who believes that the Bible is the literal and actual Word of God. It is personal. It is as if God was talking to you face to face. It is unchanging, perfect in holiness, unerring for all eternity. This highest level of belief in God's Word is the only belief that the Bible itself endorses. This may seem harsh to some, or even close minded. Still, does it make any sense at all to believe in a God who speaks truth only some of the time? To those of us who approach the Bible with faith, we must believe that what God says is true or else none of it can be true. To us, the foolishness of God's word is the only truth we trust.

> *This highest level of belief in God's Word is the only belief that the Bible itself endorses.*

As we will see, the Bible commands us to have the utmost assurance that the Word of God is true, absolute, authoritative, and contains the actual presence of God Himself.

Who is This God Who Speaks?

If you believe the Bible is absolute and authoritative (or if you're willing to entertain the thought), then we must begin with the importance of God's speech in general. And from a Biblical perspective, that takes a little groundwork.

Let us begin by examining who the God of the Bible is. There is only one God, but He exists in three persons. We call this the Trinity. It is an incredible mystery, one we'll never fully understand this side of heaven. The persons of the Trinity are the Father, the Son, and the Holy Spirit.

Each member of the Trinity comprises the Godhead, and each is unchanging, as is the very character of God Himself. After all, If God ceased to be all powerful, then He could longer be God. If God ceased to tell the Truth, He could no longer be God. God cannot be what He is not. That is why we say that it is impossible for God to change. And if God is all powerful and speaks all truth, we ought to find out exactly why (and how) God speaks.

John Frame writes that according to Scripture, God's word is his "self expression." He states in his book The Doctrine of God, "I conclude that God's word, his speech, is an essential attribute, inseparable from God's being. It is particularly identical to the second person of the Trinity, but all three persons are involved in God's speech, and the word of God exists wherever God is."[9]

Some of what this self-expression entails is simply God's pleasure in Himself within the Trinity. This may sound bizarre, or even arrogant to some people, but we must remember that God is not a human. Why shouldn't God the Father takes pleasure in the perfections of His Son. Why shouldn't He enjoy the perfection of the Holy Spirit? In fact, if God needed anything outside of Himself to bring Him joy, He would cease to be God. Why? Because if this were true, then there would be something outside of Himself that he needs in order to be satisfied, and the Bible teaches us that God is self sufficient in every way.

In his letter to the Corinthians, Paul demonstrates just how the Holy Spirit interacts with the Trinity. He writes, "these things God has revealed to us through the Spirit. For the Spirit searches everything, even the depths of God." (1 Cor. 2:10) Why would The Spirit (being that the Holy Spirit is God) search the depths of Himself?

Notice what Jesus says in the gospel of John. "Father, I desire that they also, whom you have given me, may be with me where I am, to see my glory that you have given me because you loved me before the foundation of the world." (John 17:24)

Why would God the Father love the Son (Jesus) before the world was even formed, when the Son is also God?

Looking in scripture, we see that the Trinity is a relationship. Another way to say it is that God is a community within Himself! The Spirit searches the depths of God. The Father gives to the Son and the Son converses with the Father. Love is expressed within each member of the Trinity.

You may ask, "what does this have to do with God's words?" Look again at the above passages about the Trinity. The Spirit *searches*. The Father *gives*. The Son *receives*. And presumably, all this is communicated in and among the Trinity through some form of communication. In other words, speaking is a part of who God is. And if God is all powerful and all truthful, His speech is as perfect as He Himself is perfect. And as we see throughout Scripture, His speech isn't just words alone. When He speaks, things happen.

God Speaks with Power

At the creation of the world in Genesis, God spoke, and the world was formed. God's words always contain power to accomplish the will of God who spoke them. Frame says "...his speech, like all his actions, will express his lordship attributes: his control, authority, and presence."[10]

Throughout the scriptures, when God speaks, things happen. Consider these examples of the power contained within God's speech:

> "For he spoke, and it came to be; he commanded, and it stood firm." (Psalm 33:9)

> "By the word of the Lord the heavens were made, and by the breath of his mouth all their host." (Psalm 33:6)

> "...who gives life to the dead and calls into existence the things that do not exist." (Rom. 4:17)

It is impossible for God to speak without power and authority. Thats right, its impossible. We humans sometimes say things that we do not mean. Sometimes we say things that come across different than we actually intended. Sometimes we communicate poorly. Other times we say things semi-firmly because we have a low level of conviction on a particular topic. (For example, we tell our kids semi-firmly to do the dishes, whereas we tell them emphatically not to steal.) God does not communicate this way. Everything God says contains perfect forethought, perfect intentionality, perfect holiness, and absolute power.

Whenever God creates, He *speaks* it into being. He says "let there be light," and there is light (Genesis 1:3). When God speaks, His limitlessness is contained within His words. His words carry His creative and authoritative power.

God Speaks to Man

The Scriptures show us that men are not self-sufficient. They do not contain all truth, and in fact, they are often persuaded by lies. We all know the story of the Garden of Eden, how an enemy crept into the garden in the form of a snake and drew men away from God with a lie. In following that lie, a great chasm opened, a division between needy humankind and an all-powerful, all-loving God. How can this be fixed?

God's plan and purpose is to bring redemption to mankind. How does God enact that plan? Through *speaking*. If God had not spoken to man, then we could not have known Him. God reveals Himself through His words.

We see the most direct form of redemptive speaking by God the Father when God Himself speaks directly to to His people, Israel. In Exodus 20 all of Israel is gathered around Mt. Sinai to hear the words of God. God begins to speak and declares His covenant with them and how they should serve Him. However, God's voice was so frightening and the people were so afraid of God that they begged Moses to talk to God for them so they do not die. Moses accepted the proposition, and so, God spoke directly to Moses and Moses spoke to the people.

God continued this sort of speaking arrangement through Moses for years to come. In fact, God said,

> I will raise up for them a prophet like you from among their brothers. And I will put my words in his mouth, and he shall speak to them all that I command him. And

whoever will not listen to my words that he shall speak in my name, I myself will require it of him."
(Deut. 18:18-19)

Remember, the people were so frightened of God that they wanted a prophet, a mediator between them and God. Here we see what God says, that He will put his *words* in the mouth of the prophet. Frame notes that this carries two implications:

> (1) the prophet's words are God's words (v. 18); and (2) God's words in the mouth of the prophet are fully authoritative, so that God will discipline anyone who 'refuses to listen' (v. 19)." [11]

Note also the Words of God in Exodus 4:15-16,

> You (Moses) shall speak to him (Aaron) and put the words (God's words to Moses) in his mouth, and I will be with your mouth and with his mouth and will teach you both what to do. He shall speak for you to the people, and he shall be your mouth, and you shall be as God to him.

How important is it to God that His words are authoritative? Even when God speaks to us through a mediator such as Moses, He expects us to hear the words as if it were God Himself. If God says the prophets' words are God's, then should we agree?

We see a similar importance of the authoritative word of God through the prophets. Consider the calling of Jeremiah:

> Then the Lord put out his hand and touched my mouth. And the Lord said to me, 'Behold, I have put my words in your mouth. See, I have set you this day over nations and over kingdoms, to pluck up and to break down, to destroy and to overthrow, to build and to plant.'

(Jeremiah 1:4-12)

Isn't this astonishing? First, God touches Jeremiah's mouth and gives Jeremiah *His words (God's words)*. Then God's promises His authoritative power will come through those words by causing them to build up or tear down kingdoms. Ask yourself: What man can speak on his own authority and control kingdoms? Again, the words of the prophet are are God's words. Full of authority and absolute power.

God Doesn't Just Speak to Prophets

In the New Testament, another prophet (not just any prophet) speaks the words of God, but in a new way. In Jesus Christ we have what the Bible calls a prophet, priest, and king. Even more, though, we have the earthly expression of God himself, the second person of the Trinity. And while on the earth, Jesus speaks "the words of life." How do we know they were words of life? Because they were God's own words. Consider the words of Jesus himself, recorded by the apostle John:

> For I have not spoken on my own authority, but the Father who sent me has himself given me a commandment—what to say and what to speak. (**John 12:49**)

First, notice that Jesus recognizes that words carry authority. In this passage, we see that Jesus, as a prophet, believes in the authority of God's words, and he shows us that by speaking only what the Father tells him. This means Jesus's words are authoritative because they are the very words of God.

What's more, He entrusted the disciples of Jesus to give eye witness accounts of those *words of life*, and he promised to empower them to speak with authority. In the book of John, Jesus promises his disciples that they will be carriers of his words. He says, "But the Helper, the Holy Spirit, whom the Father will send in my name, he will teach you all things and bring to your remembrance all that I have said to you." (John 14:26)

The Holy Spirit—the third member of the Trinity—will help the disciples remember Jesus's words. His saving words. His words of redemption. His life-giving words.

And after Jesus's death, after his resurrection, he was even more explicit, giving them a very clear command:

> Go therefore and make disciples of all nations, baptizing them in the name of the Father and of the Son and of the Holy Spirit, teaching them to observe all that I have commanded you. And behold, I am with you always, to the end of the age." (Matt, 28:19-20)

And this is exactly what they did. As part of that teaching, they wrote the story and the words of Jesus and shared letters with young Christians across the known world. It's this collection of stories and letters that we now call the New Testament.

On this very point, some object. Surely if Jesus was indeed God, he could have written his words down, right? But Jesus, fully understanding the power of the Spirit who would speak through the disciples, trusted the authority of his own words to be in the testimony of the disciples mouths. He knew the apostles would not spin the truth, but would faithfully communicate the words of God. On this point the apostle Peter wrote,

> Knowing this first of all, that no prophecy of Scripture comes from someone's own interpretation. For no prophecy was ever produced by the will of man, but men spoke from God as they were carried along by the Holy Spirit." (2 Peter 1:20-21)

The words of the apostles were not their own. Instead, they were God's very words! And the truth of those words would set men free!

All of this laboring comes down to this: for those who believe in Jesus and that He is Lord, It is altogether illogical to disbelieve that the Bible is the absolute authoritative word of God. You would have to be open to the possibility that the writers of the Bible were not only wrong, but that Jesus himself was wrong. And you'd have to believe that Jesus's words to his disciples were not from the Father, but rather, were nothing more than human words. You'd have to conclude that the apostles were liars, and that God in his perfect plan did not foresee the possibility that men would interpret His words incorrectly.

For the Christian, we do not have the right to water down the very words that God himself insist are "God-breathed." These words carry His power, authority, and His presence. To deny His words are to deny Him! And in fact, it would make more sense to disbelieve in Jesus altogether than to believe that he is God but misspoke or misunderstood the Father, or that he didn't know what he was doing when he tasked his followers to write his words.

If this is all true, questions arise. If the words of God are true, then why don't humans inherently recognize the truth of them? Why aren't we good enough to see them as the words of a good and loving God? Maybe at the crux of it all is this question: Why can't we know how to live righteously on our own, without the absolute truth of the God's Word?

CHAPTER 4:
I'M AN ORIGINAL

Am I capable of finding truth on my own?

"**JOHN, DON'T** touch this stove when it's red like this! Red means *hot*. It'll burn you."

It was a simple instruction from my mother, but my 4-year old brain couldn't help but question her authority.

How does my mom know if it will burn me or not? Maybe she's wrong. Maybe she's lying. Maybe what is hot to her isn't hot for me!

You've likely guessed how this story ends. Yes, I touched it. Yes, it burned. And yes, I experienced the truth for myself. I was not immune to the immutable truths of the stovetop. If I touched what was hot, I'd be burned. (And for what it's worth, my mom was also right about what would happen if I stuck my finger in the light socket.)

I knew my mom loved me and wanted to keep me from hurting myself. But I guess I wanted to experience things for myself because, after all, I was not a robot. I was not a clone. I was an original John Cooper, and maybe I was different!

It is true: I am an original, and so are you. We are capable of thinking and feeling for ourselves. God didn't create us to be stupid, right? He gave us the ability to reason. So, why do I choose the wrong path? Why do I have to touch the hot stove? Why do I believe there is a hidden truth within myself?

This leads to a pivotal point in our discussion. If I can find truth within myself—particularly, truth apart from authority—then that must mean that I was either born good, or at the least I am born into the possibility of being good. Most people believe that they were born good. As we will see, nothing could be further from the truth! Our natural bent will always be towards unrighteousness.

> *Most people believe that they were born good. As we will see, nothing could be further from the truth!*

Unrighteousness separates us from God's eternal truth. And as a foundational matter, if we attempt to depart from His truth, we'll find nothing but pain.

Uniquely Created, but the Rules Still Apply

God is an artist who loves to create. He doesn't have to create out of some need for something He doesn't already have. After all, as we've already established, He is completely self-sufficient. Instead, God enjoys creating, and He creates with wisdom and beauty and according to His sovereign will. And His creation—including us—is always individually unique.

The book of Psalms gives us an idea of how God creates us uniquely.

> "For you formed my inward parts; you knitted me together in my mother's womb." (Psalm 139:13)

The way we look, the way we think, our personalities, and our lives are original and special to God. Still, there are some things that are true about every human who has ever lived. So while we'd like to think we are absolutely one of a kind in every aspect, that kind of thinking is pride (a characteristic also common to humans).

Every one of us is a child of Adam, the first man God created. And tragically, as we will see, everyone of us is born into sin as a result of our first father's sin. In other words, all of us have disregarded our mother's instruction at one point or another; all of us have touched the stove. Why? Because each of us carries the DNA of the original man, Adam. Unfortunately, with Adam's DNA comes the curse of Adam's original sin.

Those Kids

Having kids is a serious job. Before we had our first child—Alexandria—Korey and I would go to a restaurant, a public park, a mall, or *anywhere*, and we'd notice the super-annoying, screaming kids who disobeyed their parents' pleas to quiet down. We'd look at each other, both thinking, "Our kids will NEVER be like THOSE kids!"

Guess what?

We weren't exempt.

When we had Alexandria (who immediately went by Alex), she was so innocent, so sweet, and absolutely adorable. She was unique, different than all the other kids. And so, imagine my surprise when innocent Alex turned out to be no different than all "those" other kids.

Korey and I took Alex to the Mall of America in Minneapolis. It's a massive space, and in the center there is a roller coasters and all sorts of child rides. I'll never forget how much she loved those rides, screaming, laughing and shouting, "Again! Again!" I responded, "Okay, but we have to get off now and get back in line." The mood-swing from utter joy to utter anger was beyond startling. In fact, it was horrifying! It felt like watching a horror film where the cute little girl gets possessed by something evil. Alex threw her head backwards and contorted in ways that were unnatural to the human body. It was all I could do to carry her out, all the while thinking, "I bet some of the people watching us are thinking 'MY child will NEVER be one of THOSE kids'."

My second child, Xavier, was no different. I remember an instance when my wife Korey lightly smacked his hand when he was touching something he wasn't supposed to. Two-year old Xavier looked Korey dead in the eye and smacked her right back! He'd turned out to be just as stubborn, just as rebellious, and just as capable of throwing a tantrum as any other kid. Why? Because he's just like me! He was born with the same sinful stuff we're all born with.

Anyone who believes that we are born inherently righteous need not look any further than the fruit of their own children. Set any two kids from anywhere in the world together in one room, but only give them one toy to share, and see what happens. And if you don't have children, just take a look at the world around you. Does humankind seem to be getting better, kinder, more graceful? Not if you ask me. The world seems to be nothing more than grownup children, throwing tantrums and asserting their own will. And it's getting worse by the day.

It is natural, of course, to assert our will. In fact, it was natural for Xavier to smack Korey. And though we live in a culture that teaches that natural impulses are always good, this cannot be true. Should we dismiss our own tantrums, our own hateful actions because they are natural? Or does the fact that they are natural propose a deeper problem?

All of this begs the question: If we know that not all of our natural impulses are good, why do we so often trust them? Put another way, why do we need to touch the hot stove for ourselves?

To understand our common depravity as humans, we must go back a long way. From the beginning, humans wanted to be autonomous. We desire self-governance. We want to be our own God. And from a Scriptural standpoint, this desire didn't start with man. It started in the angelic world. The theologian, Louis Berkhof writes in his systematic theology,

> Very little is said about the sin that caused the fall of the angels. From Paul's warning to Timothy, that no novice should be appointed as bishop, 'lest being puffed up he fall into the condemnation of the devil,' 1 Tim. 3:6, we may in all probability conclude that it was the sin of pride, of aspiring to be like God in power and authority.[12]

Traditional Christian teaching holds that Satan wanted to be like God. He wanted the glory, the authority, and the worship that belonged only to God. He rebelled against God because he wanted autonomy and self-governance. Berkhof continues,

> ..it is said that the fallen angels 'kept not their own principality, but left their proper habitation.' They were not satisfied with their lot, with the government and power entrusted to them. If the desire to be like God was their first peculiar temptation, this would also explain why they tempted man on that particular point.[13]

Satan and the fallen angels rebelled against God by desiring autonomy. Is it any surprise that he tempted mankind with the same desire?

You may recall the story of Adam and Eve. They were placed in the Garden of Eden and were given explicit instructions by God: "[Do] not to eat fruit from the trees in the middle of the garden, and you must not touch it, or you will die"(Gen. 3:2-3). God warned Adam and Eve. In essence, he said, "the stove is hot." But did that stop Satan from trying to tempt them? Of course not. Instead, he took the form of a serpent and told Eve that she would not die if she ate the fruit. In fact, he said,"God knows that when you eat from it your eyes will be opened, and you will be like God, knowing good and evil" (Gen. 3:4-5).

You know what happened. Eve succumbed to temptation, and subsequently tempted Adam to eat the forbidden fruit, even though they had such a clear instruction from God not to do it. Eve believed the serpent. She believed that there was truth to be found outside of God's word.

Regarding Adam and Eve's sinful choice, Matthew Henry writes, "[T]his act involved disbelief in God's word, together with confidence in the devil's, discontent with his present state, pride in his own merits, and ambition of the honor which comes not from God, envy at God's perfections, and indulgence of the appetites of the body."[14] In other words, Adam and Eve were not content to be human. They wanted to be like God. They desired to make their own decisions. They believed they could figure out what was best for them through their own reasoning.

Does this sound familiar? It should! This is what we all do!

Each of us has wrestled with the desire to be self governing. But our desire for autonomy is not only the same desire that caused the

> *When you and I choose to believe ourselves instead of believing God's word, we are committing the same sin that Satan committed.*

fall of Adam and Eve, but is also the same desire that caused the fall of Lucifer from the angelic world. And In case it is not clear, let me state it pointedly: When you and I choose to believe ourselves instead of believing God's word, we are committing the same sin that Satan committed. Yes, that's right. When we sin, we are acting like Satan.

The hard truth demonstrated by the scriptures is this: We are born in a natural state of the flesh, and without intervention, we'll act exactly like our father Adam (and his deceiver, the Devil).

So What is Original Sin?

Speaking to the religious leaders of his day, Jesus said, "You are of your father the devil, and you want to do the desires of your father" (John 8:44). Jesus's words were clear. Those religious leaders were simply living out the corruption passed down to them by their forefather Adam.

Adam is our first father, but he is also the representative head of all his descendants. His one original sin of disobedience set off a tragic chain reaction that would effect every single human being that would ever be born. His sin begets our sin. We cannot escape it, we cannot run from it. We are born into it.

King David knew this truth. He wrote, "For I was born a sinner-yes, from the moment my mother conceived me" (Psalm 51:5). And this was not to say that he was forced to sin (by sleeping with Bathsheba, for instance). Instead, his choice to sin grew from his sinful nature, the nature passed down from Adam.

Berkhof writes regarding Adam's first sin,

> That sin carried permanent pollution with it, and a pollution which, because of the solidarity of the human race, would affect not only Adam but all his descendants as well. As a result of the fall the father of the race could only pass on a depraved human nature to his offspring. From that unholy source sin flows on as an impure stream to all the generations of men, polluting everyone and everything with which it comes in contact.[15]

This was a truth that David understood. And implicitly, it's a truth so many of us understand, too.

This permanent pollution of all of mankind has immediate ramifications. First, all of of us are born into a nature of depravity. Secondly, and more tragic, our communion with God is broken, which causes both physical and spiritual death. In other words, we've got *big* problems.

From its earliest pages, the Scriptures teach the truth of humankind's depravity. In fact, just before the great flood in the age of Noah, the Bible states, "The Lord observed the extent of human wickedness on the earth, and he saw that everything they thought or imagined was consistently and totally evil" (Genesis 6:5). Totally evil. Totally depraved. All the time.

We live in a time when humanity no longer thinks of ourselves "totally evil." In fact, many see the natural state of humankind as morally good. Many believe that if we were only given the right amount of information, we would make righteous decisions.

Nothing could be farther from the truth. We see this truth throughout Bible, but the history of mankind evidences it, too. We are capable of the greatest evil, and we pursue violence as sport. Humankind has perpetuated great genocides—against Jews, rival ethnic groups, and even babies in the womb. We are driven by our unending hunger for power. Our appetites—for food, sex, wealth, or power—are insatiable. Our creativity in finding new ways to sin is infinite. And it's this infinite capacity for sin that flows from the original sin of Adam.

John Calvin set out to describe our innate capacity for sin. He wrote, "Original sin, then, may be defined a hereditary corruption and depravity of our nature, extending to all the parts of the soul, which first makes us obnoxious to the wrath of God, and then produces in us works which in Scripture are termed works of the flesh."[16]

Hold up," you might be saying. "What if sin isn't passed down through the spiritual genes? What if it's learned? Couldn't we somehow *unlearn* it?" It's a fair question, one resolved by the Bible. In his letter to the Romans, the apostle Paul wrote, "And I know that nothing good lives in me, that is, in my flesh. I want to do what is right, but I can't. I want to do what is good, but I don't. I don't want to do what is wrong, but I do it anyway" (Rom. 7:18-19).

In case anyone thinks that perhaps Paul was only talking about himself, rest assured, he was not. In fact, just a few chapters earlier he all but quoted Psalm 14, where the psalmist writes, "[T]he Lord looks down from heaven on the entire human race; he looks to see if anyone is truly wise, if anyone seeks God. But no, all have turned away; all have become corrupt, no one does good, not a single one!" (Psalm 14:2-3).

We have been born into the slavery of sin, and the painful result of this spiritual slavery is both spiritual death, but also physical death. Paul said as much, again writing to the Romans that "the wages of sin is death" (Rom 6:23a). There was good news, though. Paul continued, "but the gift of God is eternal life" (Rom. 6:23b).

Without an intervention, we will remain in sin. We'll continue to chase our desires, to hurt our neighbors, to do what it takes to get a leg up. As a result, we'll remain in spiritual death. This is so different than what we hear in society these days. Our current culture tells us we are good, that we have truth in our hearts, and that we should follow it. If we do, we'll follow it all the way to the death.

Is it Possible to Beat Sin by Living a Good Life?

Some may ask, "what if I live a good life? Can I beat this whole original sin thing?" The Bible gives a clear answer. It teaches that without God, we are incapable of being righteous. And besides, we all know that when we do good things, the intent of our heart is often to receive a little bit of glory. (This sounds an awful lot like self-worship, doesn't it?) The Bible refers to this kind of righteousness as "filthy rags." (Isaiah 64:6). In Isaiah's days, these "filthy rags" referred to the cloths used by women during their menstrual cycles.

We cannot possibly be righteous or holy on our own merit. In this sense, there is no such thing as a good person.

Of course, this doesn't mean that it's impossible for someone to commit a good act, such as feeding the poor, or having integrity in business dealings, or not cheating on your taxes. However, there is a difference between doing good and being righteous. As we've seen, even when we do good, we're still infected by the desire to sin. And though that desire might start in the heart, it spread to every part of the body. Again, Berkhof writes, "And from this center (the heart) its (sin) influence and operations spread to the intellect, the will, the affections, in short, to the entire man, including his body. In his sinful state the whole man is the object of God's displeasure."[17]

In short, because of our original state of sin, we cannot do anything but displease God. We cannot win Him over with our good deeds, because even those are tainted. In fact, the only reason that we do not constantly act as thoroughly depraved as possible is because of God's common grace that restrains us from our very worst leanings and intentions. Without the restraining grace of God over mankind, our natural state would be one of animalistic barbarianism, fulfilling every evil desire in our minds, desires placed by our own flesh and by Satan himself. If you are looking for evidence of a gracious God, look no further than the fact that we are not living in hell on earth.

Wow, John—You're Bumming me Out.

Perhaps you think this is depressing. Truth is, I hope you do. Why? Because we must deeply understand how tragic the fall of man was in order to deeply understand the triumph of God over our sin nature. In our pursuit of absolute truth, it is imperative to understand that our desire for self governance has led us to a place of rebellion against God. And this means that we are spiritually dead. The only hope we have to understanding and recognizing truth is for us to somehow become spiritually alive. Is this possible? If our hearts are darkened and evil, then is there a way to be given a brand new heart?

The answer to both of these questions is a resounding "yes!" Soon, we will see that God offers us a brand new heart, and a brand new nature that is not corrupt. He offers us life eternal, and so much more! But before we begin to talk about the great news of the gift of God, we must continue to explore the incredible deficits of mankind when it comes to looking for truth.

"Wait, it gets worse?" You may ask.

At this point, you may object. Maybe you'd say "Okay John, I understand that man is not born 'good.' But this doesn't mean that every action I take is a result of my desire for self-governance and autonomy. Don't my emotions play a part in showing me what is right? Certainly, God gave me emotions for a reason, didn't He?"

Take a look around you. Look on the TV. Look on social media. Look at the hate, the rage, the violence, the bigotry. This is what it looks like when all of us as individuals follow our own emotions. The unfortunate truth is, you can't always trust your feelings. Why? Because as we'll see, our feelings are the product of our fallen nature, too.

CHAPTER 5:
SIMPLY IRRESISTIBLE

Can my emotions lead me to the truth?

"JOHN, I'M gonna tell Stacey that God told me she's the one. We are going to get married."

My jaw dropped to the floor. So many thoughts raced into my head that I didn't know which one to bring up first. Without formulating any sort of clear argument, I opted for a rapid fire approach.

"Dude, don't do that! You don't know her. She doesn't know you. You're eight years older than her. I think she's still a teenager? She's going to think you are a psycho because you *are* a psycho. And in case you forgot, this is the third girl that God has supposedly told you that you were going to marry."

I felt like he was on the Titanic, but only I saw the impending iceberg. But try as I may, he wouldn't listen. He continued on until the relationship ended just as one would suspect. In fact, it ended the same way the Titanic did. It was a shipwreck of a relationship.

Most of us have experienced some version of this story, and we all know how it ends. Why are we so stubborn about the things *we just know that we know*? Even when our track record for being wrong far outweighs the times we have actually been right, it never seems to shake our confidence.

Of course, there have been countless times in my life when the roles were reversed and I was the one in self-denial, headed toward the metaphorical iceberg. Resolute, I've held fast to many things that I believed were true but in the end brought me nothing but pain and loss because they were not in line with God's Word. Why did I believe them?

When you believe something with such absolute certainty, it is difficult to imagine you could be wrong. This is why men keep chasing women who've told them *no* time and time again. It's why people buy lottery tickets week after week, sure that one day, they'll hit the jackpot and be set for life. It's why some who believe they'll never get cancer keep smoking cigarettes.

In my profession, I meet a great many people who feel called to be musicians. I always want to encourage them, because having a dream is a powerful thing. And sometimes, those musicians make it, even the ones I least suspect. Sometimes God has plans that don't make sense (at least, not to me). Still, the truth is, no matter how hard a person believes, the likelihood of a 50 year old dude finally finding his big break in rock music is extremely slim. Especially in this fallen society where the market is much bigger for pop music than it is for rock music. (God save us. I truly believe this is a sign of the times.)

Sometimes, the truths people believe are absolutely gut wrenching. Consider my friend, (a confessing Christian) who was convinced he should leave his wife and four children for another woman who was destined to be his true soul mate. "Why would I have these feelings if it wasn't meant to be?" he asked. No matter how many people pled with him to see the truth of God's Word, he continued to hold fast to his belief. He openly agreed that the Bible commands faithfulness within marriage. He openly agreed that the Bible commands him to care for his family. Still, he claimed, "this is different because I was *meant* to be with this new woman." How do you argue with that?

In this tragic true story, my friend's belief had very little to do with the actual truth, the truth that he knew. Still, he was completely convinced of the rightness of his feelings, and it destroyed his marriage. It destroyed his kids. It destroyed their friends, their community, and their extended family. And this is so often the tragic end of following your feelings.

MUTUALLY ASSURED SELF DESTRUCTION

Our feelings can be the biggest obstacle in our search for truth. In fact, we can become so convinced by our feelings that they become *convictions*. And convictions are difficult things to overcome. In fact, our convictions are so powerful, that even when they are at odds with the truth, we find it nearly impossible to believe that truth.

> *Our feelings can be the biggest obstacle in our search for truth.*

Our desire to live autonomously often results in us making judgements based on our *irresistible convictions*. By 'irresistible convictions' I am not talking about foundational principles. Nor am I talking about convictions based on the Bible, parental wisdom, or societal values. Instead, our irresistible convictions often flow from the feelings and emotions that motivate and animate you.

Remember the story about my mother telling me not to touch the hot stove, and my irresistible need to see for myself just how hot it was? Part of the reason for this was my conviction that I knew better. I knew my mom was serious. I wasn't just rebellious. Instead, I believed the stove would not hurt me. My belief was so strong that I couldn't help but believe myself over her. You might even say I could not resist the pull to believe the inner voice. It was my irresistible conviction that led me to believe that the stove would not burn me.

The Christian is called to follow the Word of God as the ultimate source of truth. Not occasionally. Not just when we want to. Not just when we agree with the Bible or when our feelings line up with the teachings of the Bible. Part of building your house upon the rock is understanding that your personal feelings do not always line up with the truth of God. When this happens, the one who builds his life on the rock will follow God's truth over their feelings.

When I had my first child, I was prepared to discipline her. I understood that if you teach a child to have respect early on in life it benefits her for her entire life. I also understood that there would be times when Korey and I might have to punish her. And when that time came, I understood what my dad meant when he used to say, "this hurts me more than it hurts you." I still laugh about the first time Korey spanked our daughter. Alex didn't even cry, but Korey did!

Like any parent, there have been times when I just didn't want to discipline my children. I might have been too tired from all the obligations of life. I might have been too tired from constantly disciplining them. Still, even though I didn't *feel* like punishing them, the Word of God—my ultimate truth—required it. So, I disciplined my kids based on what the Bible says and not on how I felt in the moment.

How's that worked out for us?

Over the last seventeen years, our kids have been on tour with Skillet. And without fail, every tour ends with our fellow bandmates and friends complimenting our kids behavior and asking how we raised such amazing kids. Time and time again, I tell them we chose God's way of discipline, even when it cut against our feelings, even when I didn't want to. And as a result, I get to live in the blessings of obedience!

What applies to raising children applies to so many other areas of life, too. We can follow our feelings when it comes to sexuality or drug addiction or pornography addiction or lying or a failing marriage or whatever. And a further truth is, a great many horrors have been committed on this earth due to humans "following their hearts" instead of the undeniable truth. Consider the dictators, murderers, serial killers, and all sorts of heinous criminals who believed in the unquestionable rightness of what they were doing, even when it involved the slaughter of innocent people.

Charles Hodge sums up the end of following our feelings, writing,

> Thousands have been, and still are, fully convinced that the false is true, and that what is wrong is right. To tell men, therefore, to look within for an authoritative guide, and to trust to their irresistible convictions, is to give them a guide which will lead them to destruction.[18]

And if we all follow our own unique feelings, there's only one logical conclusion. We will not only live in anarchy, but eventually in mutually assured self-destruction.

Out of Alignment

This leads to an obvious question: are emotions bad? Absolutely not! Imagine a world without emotion. Without the love of your life. Without the joy of eating ice cream with your kids. Even without the sorrow that makes pleasure so much more joyful. See? Emotion is a wonderful gift from God.

Emotion is not evil. Far from it! Emotion was God's gift to us. In fact, God has emotions. As we have already discussed, God takes pleasure in Himself. He expresses His joy to Himself within the relationship of the Trinity. God also takes pleasure in His people! Consider the words of the prophet Zephaniah, "The Lord your God is in your midst, a mighty one who will save; he will rejoice over you with gladness; he will quiet you by his love; he will exult over you with loud singing" (Zeph. 3:17).

The God of the Bible is not apathetic to the world. He is not far away and unaware of our daily struggles. He sings loudly over us! He is emotional about his people! The Bible also compares God to a bridegroom who rejoices over his bride, which is His people (Isaiah 62:5). God is altogether passionate and expressive with His Church and He enjoys all of His creation.

As we see, emotion is a wonderful gift from God! But trouble arises because unlike God, we are not perfect. In an email addressed to me, Dr. James White says, "Obviously, God does not experience emotion as creatures do, where often the emotion arises out of impurity, selfishness, past sin, shame, etc. God's rejoicing, or His wrath, etc., flow in perfect harmony from His nature, so that He is not changed by outside forces or unexpected emotional responses." We are human, and therefore our humanity extends to every part of us. Remember, the curse of original sin is pervasive, infecting every single aspect of our lives, including our emotions. We are inherently selfish. All of our natural emotional leanings are self-driven for the end goal of our flesh, which is to live autonomously. This is why our emotions drive irresistible convictions that are not aligned with the truth.

How Our Emotions Compete with the Spirit

Some Christians ask, "if my heart has been made new by God, then won't my heart tell me what is right and wrong?" In other words, can't we trust our emotions after we follow Christ? This is a complicated question.

The Bible says "When the Spirit of truth comes, he will guide you into all the truth, for he will not speak on his own authority, but whatever he hears he will speak, and he will declare to you the things that are to come" (John 16:13). Is this proof that as long as we've trusted in Christ and have the Spirit we are safe to trust our emotions? Again, let's turn to Charles Hodge, who writes of relying solely on the Spirit inside of us as evidence of truth: "The inward teaching and testimony of the Spirit are Scriptural truths, and truths of inestimable value. But it is ruinous to put them in the place of the divinely authenticated written Word."[19]

Hodge's point? While it is wonderful that we have the Holy Spirit inside of us to guide us, we must not let the Spirit overrule the written Word. And to be clear, this does not mean that the Spirit would actually speak anything contradictory to the written Word. Rather, humans are prone to misinterpret what the Spirit says, or misunderstand or even imagine that the Spirit is saying something that He is not. Why? Because our emotions and desires often compete with the Truth of God. In fact, the prophet Isaiah wrote, "For my thoughts are not your thoughts, neither are your ways my ways, declares the Lord" (Isaiah 55:8).

I have noticed this with a great many Christians. Some have been friends, some have been fellow members of the same local church congregation , and some have been public figures such as pastors, influencers, or worship leaders. What I have noticed is that some of these people confessed to loving Jesus—and they believed that it was real because they *felt* a love for Jesus. They were "on fire" for Jesus. Professing their love for Jesus gave them a feeling of hope, joy, and peace during their trials. I personally think it's a wonderful thing to get emotional about Jesus because His death on the cross has set me free. It is right to sing and shout and celebrate! The problem is not that we are emotional about our faith, but when our faith is based on our emotions. What happens when the emotion wanes? What happens when life doesn't work out the way we had hoped or prayed? No matter how much we shout that we love Jesus, if we do not build our lives upon His Word we will be shattered by the inevitable waves of our sinful desires. Let me say something that may shock you— the Christian who does not know what God loves and hates is in danger of believing that God approves of evil things. Time after time I have witnessed self-proclaimed Jesus-lovers follow their emotions into a path of sin, and after reaping the consequences I have watched in disbelief as they blamed God for all of their problems.

> *The problem is not that we are emotional about our faith, but when our faith is based on our emotions.*

The Bible goes to great lengths to help us understand how different God is from us. This is why it is imperative that we do not fully trust our own emotions, especially when they lead us to go against God's Word. As the prophet Jeremiah wrote, "The heart is deceitful above all things, and desperately sick; who can understand it?" (Jeremiah 17:9). The power of sin is broken over us, but we are still prone to stray, prone to want to live autonomously due to our flesh. This is the result of being trapped in our sinful bodies.

Walk in the Spirit

If we cannot trust our emotions, then how do we know if we are doing what is right? How can we know if our irresistible convictions line up with God's truth? For those who have been born again through the death of Jesus Christ, God gives us an incredible gift—The gift of the Holy Spirit!

The Holy Spirit, third person of the Trinity, is the very presence of God living inside of us, changing us from the inside out! When we abide in God and obey His Word, the Bible says we are *walking in the Spirit*. As Paul wrote to the church in Galatia,

> "But I say, walk by the Spirit, and you will not gratify the desires of the flesh. For the desires of the flesh are against the Spirit, and the desires of the Spirit are against the flesh, for these are opposed to each other, to keep you from doing the things you want to do." (Gal. 5:16-17)

Paul shows how the work of the Spirit brings deeper understanding of the Scriptures to us, which helps us avoid the harmful desires in our bodies.

There is without a doubt a battle between the flesh and the Spirit. It is real. It is painful. It is war! Often, we tend to think of this as two equal forces engaging in an epic battle, unsure of who will win. Sort of like King Kong versus Godzilla. Or Batman versus Superman. (Batman is clearly the champion). But if we believe the Word of God, this battle will seem very different to us. The victory is certain. The war is not between two opposing forces of equal military might. The war is between an omnipotent, all-powerful God and His enemy, Satan. But the only power that Satan has is the power to accuse or tempt us.

If we have been justified before God through the death of Jesus Christ, if his Spirit lives in us, then Satan can bring no accusation against us! He is silenced by Jesus Christ, the son of God who is "at the right hand of God, who indeed is interceding for us" (Rom.8:34).

Even still, we must contend with our our own desires. After all, we are still in the midst of a spiritual battle. How do we fight against our desires? We do so by saying "no" to sin. In the words of Paul, we "Put to death therefore what is earthly in you: sexual immorality , impurity, passion, evil desire, and covetousness , which is idolatry" (Col. 3:5).

In a world where the will of God seems unclear, how do we know when our emotions and desires are getting in the way? Paul gives us the answer in his letter to the Romans: "Do not be conformed to this world, but be transformed by the renewal of your mind, that by testing you may discern what is the will of

God, what is good and acceptable and perfect" (Rom. 12:2). How are we transformed? By the renewing of our minds that comes from reading, believing, and acting on the Word of God, the ultimate truth.

There will be times when the lines between wrong and right are blurred. I can guarantee it! Our emotions will cause us to believe beyond a shadow of a doubt that we should follow a path that is inconsistent with the Bible. So, we should be on guard at all times, clinging to the truth of the Word of God.

LORD OF OUR EMOTIONS

God has created us with the gift of emotions, and life is all the sweeter because of it! But those wonderful emotions cannot be our foundation for living. Where do they belong? We must put our emotions and feelings under the Lordship of Jesus and the truth of His Word. So let us walk in step with the Spirit and resist our *irresistible convictions* of our desires and emotions when they conflict with God's Word. At this point, I think that most people would agree that we should be on guard against our emotions. However, I believe that our culture's relativism has affected us more deeply than we know. Is it possible that Christians have been shaped by worldly philosophies that *felt* like truth but are actually at war against God? Could this have happened without us even realizing it? If we are to find truth, we must take a bold step and look at the prevailing irresistible conviction that is plaguing both society and the church at the moment.

CHAPTER 6:
LOVE IS NOT GOD

If God is love, Can I find truth by being a loving person?

A FRIEND OF mine came to me, told me his dear friends were going through a divorce. They'd been married for years and had kids, he said, but the husband had been having an affair with another man. So, the man left his wife for his new lover.

It was all so awful, he said, but it wasn't the most concerning part. What was worse? The wife had told him that she'd accepted her husband's decision, and in fact, was attempting to be happy for him. Happy for him? Huh?

I was stunned. Shocked. More shocking? She said that if her husband had cheated on her with another woman, it would be unforgivable. However, since he was just coming to terms with his truest self, she felt the loving thing to do was to accept him, support him, and even be happy for him. But does allowing someone to break a vow because their sexual appetites have changed sound like love to you?

It's a story that exposes a bigger issue, I think. In a relativistic world, how can we define love?

We live in a culture so self-consumed and so focused on our own desires that we do not realize how ridiculous our idea of love is. This is responsible for much of the chaos and confusion in the world and in the Church alike.

The scriptures says simply, "God is love" (1 John 4:8). Unfortunately, though, this verse is becoming the foundation of all sorts of wrong thinking, heresy, and even apostasy. But as we will see in this chapter, God defines love, not us. And as A. W. Tozer so boldly taught, God is love, but love is not God.

THE CULTURE OF LOVE?

When I was growing up, it was cheesy to talk about love all of the time, particularly among men. In fact, just one generation or so ago, many fathers did not often say "I love you" to their own children. Perhaps this is an exaggeration, but as a generalization, many fathers felt uncomfortable using the phrase. Did this mean fathers didn't love their children? Hardly. In those days, many father's demonstrated love by taking care of the family's needs.

What do I mean?

When I was growing up, a father might say, "I don't need to tell him I love him. He knows it. I put food on the table and clothes on his back." This may seem very old fashioned to some people, especially in today's society, and I'm not saying I endorse it. There has to be a balance. In fact, I don't think a single day has passed when I have not told my kids that I love them.

Today, it's all very different. You can't walk into a gas station without seeing the word "love" on product packaging or magazines in the checkout line. You go to yoga to show self love. When you end a workout session, your instructor tells you to stretch to show your body some love. Love—it's what makes a Subaru (though I never understood this). Recently, I saw a "show yourself unconditional love" campaign, which seemed super bizarre. Up until about five minutes ago (give or take), the only people who ever talked about unconditional love were religious people, and we were mocked for it.

The Bible speaks of the way God loves us, sometimes using the word "agape" to express that type of love. Agape is unconditional love. It is a love not based on emotion, therefore it doesn't fade with bad behavior nor does it burn brighter with good behavior. It is self-sacrificing love.

Christians sometimes use the phrase "agape love" within a religious context because fellow believers understand that it is miraculous that God would love us in this extraordinary way. Furthermore we understand that it separates how wonderful and different God is to humans because we do not naturally have the capacity to truly love someone perfectly and without condition.

Today, every workout guru, social media influencer, nutritionist, and life coach proudly preaches that we must have agape love... wait for it... for *ourselves*. It should be noted that I've yet to see any life coaches say that we should have agape love for *others*. This begs the question: For all this talk about love, are we really more loving as a society?

ARE WE FAILING AT LOVE

Trying to measure whether or not society is more loving now than two generations ago might seem simple if you only look at emotions and sentimentality.

We're quicker to say "I love you," and quicker to try to accept others out of "love." We try to show love to ourselves, even if we sometimes fail. But does this mean we're more loving as a society? Lets look at some measurements that might give us an indication.

1. Marriage and Divorce

Conservative estimates indicate the current rate of divorce is 42-46%. And though divorce rates may have declined in recent years, marriage rates are at a steep decline. The Pew Research center shows that "Half of U.S. adults today are married, a share that has remained relatively stable in recent years but is down 9 percentage points over the past quarter of a century and dramatically different from the peak of 72% in 1960 to 50% in 2017."[20] In fact, according to a recent article, marriage rates fell to "the lowest level in the 118-year period covered by the new report and the lowest recorded since 1867, the first year for which federal government data on national marriage is available."[21]

This makes clear that marriage rates are at the lowest point in American history. People are getting married later in life and sometimes never. And according to the research, this is not only due to the inability to find the right partner or not having enough money. It is also due to the fact that people seem more interested in their careers than in marriage. A 2019 poll indicates that "nearly two-thirds of Americans (65%) say society is just as well off if people have priorities other than marriage and having children—a significant increase from the 57% who said this in 2016."[22]

Stunning. Modern Americans prioritize their own careers over participation in an age-old institution, one that brings stability to society and produces the next generation.

2. A Declining Birth Rate

We are procreating less. The statistics of children being born in America "have dropped for the fifth year in a row, reaching a new low for the past 35 years."[23] Truth be told, there are are many reasons for the declining birth rates. We live in uncertain economic times. People are slower to get married, which means families start later in life. The turbulent state of the world also makes people think twice about bringing kids into it. But it should be obvious that those struggles are not unique within human history.

Amy Blackstone, a sociology professor at the University of Maine and the author of *Childfree by Choice: The Movement Redefining Family and Creating a New Age of Independence* says that some couples are choosing not to have children because of the potential environmental impact.[24] Others believe that kids will get in the way of their careers, or their romantic relationships. A recent article from the New York Times indicates, "Wanting more leisure time and personal freedom" as one of the top reasons why couples don't have children.[25] What's more, some research shows that couples believe that having children makes people less happy.[26] After all, how can you agape love yourself when you're too busy trying to agape love a child?

3. Suicide Rates

The CDC released statistics on death by suicide, which showed that in the last 17 years the suicide rate in America has risen 40%.[27] Seems odd for a society that believes that agape love for ourselves is possible. Doesn't it?

The increase in suicide rates demonstrates the truth. We are not growing in our capacity for self-love. In fact, we are only growing in our capacity for self-harm.

4. Mental Health Issues

It is not only suicide rates that speak to our lack of love. The rates of depression and mental illness are sharply on the rise. This was the case even before the COVID-19 pandemic swept the globe, and has increased even higher since. According to Mental Health America, "Youth mental health is worsening. From 2012-2017, the prevalence of past-year major Depressive Episode (MDE) increased from 8.66 percent to 13.01 percent of youth ages 12-17."[28]

Since the COVID crisis, reports of severe emotional distress have become worse. It has been noted that, "[a]ccording to a recent Kaiser Family Foundation poll, more than half of Americans—56%—reported that worry or stress related to the outbreak has led to at least one negative mental health effect."[29] The Substance Abuse and Mental Health Services Administration, which provides counseling for people facing emotional distress during times of natural and human-caused disasters, received an 891% increase in distress calls from March 2019 to March 2020.³⁰

The chaos of our time has caused many to live without any peace. Many do not feel any sense of "home" even within their own house.

> *Less people are getting married, less people are having children, more people are committing suicide, and mental health problems are on the rise. Does this seem to show we are a society growing in love?*

Less people are getting married, less people are having children, more people are committing suicide, and mental health problems are on the rise. Does this seem to show we are a society growing in love?

How Do We Measure Love

So what is true love? As I said above, the Bible says that "God is love" (1 John 4:8). Religious people and non-religious people alike will celebrate the statement "God is love." But what does that mean?

Even in the Church we get it wrong. We create our own idea of God's love. Tell me if this sounds familiar: Whatever pleases us most, whatever is most self serving, and whatever fulfills our desires MUST be what God wants for us if He really loves us. I know that I have been guilty of this. Have you? For instance, we may say, "This is my sexual desire, and if God truly loves me, then He is okay with my desire." It might be absurd, but doesn't it seem to happen all the time? We justify all sorts of behavior, saying, "God loves me just as I am."

In addition, we often apply our ideas of fairness to God's love. Don't believe me? Then consider this often stated sentiment: If God is love, how can He allow people to go to hell? Even modern Christians fall into this trap. And their logic goes something like this: (1) God is love; (2) hell is bad; (3) love isn't bad; (4) so, God wouldn't allow someone to go to hell. This childish reasoning has become dominant in the modern Church because we have come to believe that God's love must mean that He cannot judge us. In other words, many people mistakenly believe that God's love and God's holy judgment are mutually exclusive.

Yes, God is love! God loves His creation, God loves His people. God is good by nature. His love never changes. He always believes and He is always faithful. But this doesn't mean that our human concept of love *is* God. A.W. Tozer says,

> "Had the apostle declared that love is what God is, we would be forced to infer that God is what love is. If literally God is love, then literally love is God, and we are duty bound to worship love as the only God there is. If love is equal to God then God is only equal to love, and God and love are identical. Thus we destroy the concept of personality in God and deny outright all His attributes save one, and that one substitute for God."[31]

God cannot be defined in a word, particularly our finite human words. And we must never fall into the mistaken idea that one of God's attributes can cancel out another. For example the fact that I am white does not mean that I am not male. I am white, and I am male, and both go hand in hand. Both exist in me at the same time. Likewise, God is at all times love, and He is at all times perfectly righteous and just. It's His righteousness that demands sin to be punished. This is why the Bible states, "Cursed be anyone who does not confirm the words of this law by doing them.' "(Deut 27:26).

As we already know, God never lies. He hates sin! How can God be loving if He is not also full of justice? Look again to noted theologian John Frame, who writes, "God cannot love goodness without hating evil. The two are opposite sides of the same coin, positive and negative ways of describing the same virtue."[32]

> *...we must never fall into the mistaken idea that one of God's attributes can cancel out another.*

Our sins are an incredible offense against God. We are meant to be image-bearers of God. Therefore, when we fall short of imitating His perfections and His moral character, we defile His image. When we defile His image we awaken His jealous wrath. This doesn't weaken the love of God or make it any less. In fact, the opposite is true! As Frame wrote, "Without the wrath of God against those who finally disbelieve, God's love is no longer righteousness. So God's righteousness binds together his love and his wrath."[33]

This concept shouldn't be foreign to us. Do we show our "love" for the unrepentant child molester by letting him off the hook for his actions because he was being his truest self? Who will give justice—*i.e.*, show love—to the abused?

Does the man who steals from the poor escape punishment? What about the victimizer who preys on the weak? Should we demand justice for these great evils? Of course we should! No honest person would disagree.

It is only natural that we demand that sin be punished. If it was your child that had been molested, and God refused to bring punishment on the unrepentant abuser, would you think God was loving? Would you find Him to be just?

Or consider this example. Imagine your child wants to take his crayons and colors into the middle of a busy street. Would you allow him to? Of course not! What if he says that playing in the street is the only thing that makes him happy and he accuses you of being an unloving parent if you disallow it. Would you then say "Okay, I'll let you do it because I love you"? Hardly. Why? Because keeping your kids safe is loving.

And what about the parent who refuses to discipline their kids? The Bible says, "For the Lord disciplines the one he loves, and chastises every son whom he receives" (Heb. 12:6). If we as parents refuse to discipline our kids, to help show them how to live, to keep them safe and save them from harm, sin, and themselves, then do we actually love them?

WE DO NOT WORSHIP LOVE!

For a moment, imagine love. For this exercise, do not imagine the God of the Bible. Imagine a bright shining ball of light that is love. This ball of light is the essence of your ideal version of love. It gives you everything you want. It allows you to cheat on your spouse if it's what you want. It allows you to be an addict if that's what makes you happy. If you want to play in the street with your crayons, great. This shining ball of light loves each person in the world, allowing all of them autonomy to be who they are and be their truest selves.

Now, open your eyes and realize that this ball of light cannot bring justice. It can't give peace because each autonomous human being's ideal version of love is at war with others' ideal version. This idea of light and love is counterfeit. It is not real! One man's love would inspire another man's hate. One man's dream of extramarital affairs brings another woman's pain of betrayal. One man's desire to institute moral power over others is another man's infringement of personal freedoms.

This ball of light can never break the power of sin over your life, but rather it endorses the sin in your life. Why? Because if this ball of light loves you as you want, it will never bring discipline or correction. It cannot satisfy justice. Therefore, in one sense you would be living in personal freedom, but it's a personal freedom that makes you a slave to destruction.

God's Extravagant Love

This is why we must not worship love. Love is not god, but God is love! His love is kind. Forgiving. Full of mercy! The Bible describes God's love in such extreme and extravagant ways. Consider these Scriptures:

> "The steadfast love of the Lord never ceases; his mercies never come to an end; They are new every morning; great is your faithfulness" (Lamentations 3:22-23)

> "..in Christ God was reconciling the world to himself, not counting their trespasses against them" (2 Corinthians 5:19)

> "But God shows his own love for us in that while we were still sinners, Christ died for us." (Romans 5:8)

God's justice and righteousness demands that our sin be punished and that God's wrath be satisfied. Therefore, it is precisely God's love that sent Jesus to the cross to pay the price and penalty for our sins. "For our sake he made him to be sin who knew no sin, so that in him we might become the righteousness of God" (2 Corinthians 5:21). What greater love could there be than this? Jesus never sinned, but he became sin so that we sinners could become like him! This is where love and justice meet, on the bloody cross of Christ.

It is God's hatred of sin that makes His love seem even more loving. It cannot be over-stated. Therefore, we cannot fathom the infinity of God's love, nor can we fathom the infinity of God's hatred towards sin. If we rightly understand the present danger of sin and the coming judgement of God, then the love of God becomes so much more wonderful, and rightly so! After all, it is the love of God that leads captives out of death and into eternal life.

CHAPTER 7:
TEAR DOWN YOUR IDOLS

Can I choose to believe only the truths of God that I like?

IN 2010, I was on a co-headline tour across the United States. We were just beginning to air on radio stations for the first time, and even though we were starting to sell pretty well, I wasn't used to people recognizing me in public.

I was walking down the street before a soundcheck and a girl called to me, ran over, and struck up a conversation. She began crying and sharing a heart-wrenching story. My music made her feel understood, she said. And though I struggled through the shock of being recognized on the street, her story moved me. What's more, I felt honored that God would use my music to help her.

We spoke for another few minutes, and she asked to get a quick picture. I agreed, and as she was pulling out her camera, she said, "Oh my gosh I cannot believe that I finally got to meet Jacoby!"

Jacoby? The singer from Papa Roach?

I didn't know whether I should tell her the truth or let her continue to think that her dream had come true. In the end, I thought it would be better to be honest so I said, "I'm so sorry but I'm not Jacoby! But I will take a picture if you want."

Her cheeks turned bright pink. I'm sure mine did, too. And we snapped that awkward photo.

Even though it was a nice story and genuinely moving, in the end, the story had nothing to do with me. She didn't even know me. She loved me because she thought I was someone else. So, I could not appropriate her kind words, could not use them to fuel my songwriting. (In fact, I kind of wished I were Jacoby.)

How important is it that we're able to recognize God? How important is it to worship God for who He is, rather than who we would like Him to be? And if He really is the God of the universe, how important is it to love God and value Him more than we value other things in our life?

No Other Gods

There are many forms of idolatry in the Bible. What is idolatry? Let's start in with the initial concept of idolatry as written about in the Old Testament.

Most of us know the story of God giving Moses the Ten Commandments. Among those commandments, God said, "You shall have no other gods before me. You shall not make for yourself a carved image, or any likeness of anything that is in heaven above, or that is in the earth beneath, or that is in the water under the earth" (Ex. 20:3-4).

If there is only one true God, why should He give this command? Because throughout the Old Testament we see people worshipping physical idols. Sometimes they were statues made of gold. Sometimes they were relics carved of stone. There were also altars built to other pagan gods. But God commanded His people not to bow to the false Gods of the age. In fact, God sometimes commanded His people to tear down the foreign idols.

How much does God hate idolatry, though? He hates it so much it was a capital offense in the Old Testament. In the book of Deuteronomy, God instructed,

> If there is found among you, within any of your towns that the Lord your God is giving you, a man or woman who does what is evil in the sight of the Lord your God, in transgressing his covenant, and has gone and served other gods and worshipped them, or the sun or the moon or any of the host of heaven, which I have forbidden, and it is told you and you hear of it, then you shall inquire diligently, and if it is true and certain that such an abomination has been done in Israel, then you shall bring out to your gates that man or woman who has done this evil thing, and you shall stone that man or woman to death with stones. (**Deut. 17:2-5**)

Within the discussion of idols in the Old Testament, God introduces Himself as a jealous God. How is God's jealousy a good thing, particularly when we normally equate jealousy with something negative? God's jealousy is perfectly righteous (just as all his other traits). It's the kind of jealousy a husband feels for his wife, particularly if some knuckle-dragger were to hit on her. And in fact, the Bible uses marital language when talking about the relationship between God and His people.

John Frame helps us better understand God's righteous jealousy for His people. He writes, "Jealousy (Heb. qin' ah, GHk. Zelos) is a passionate zeal to guard the exclusiveness of a marriage relationship, leading to anger against an unfaithful spouse."[34] See? God wants to preserve our relationship. He wants to be our first love and greatest passion. God desires to be worshipped supremely by His people. And when we do not worship Him supremely, we awaken His jealous wrath.

We Idolize What We Value Supremely

The most obvious form of idolatry is worshipping an object rather than God. Expanding the concept of an idol, however, brings the issue much closer to home. For most people today, worshipping a physical object is not a temptation. The primary idolatry of the day is some passion or person over God.

We see this expansive understanding in the New Testament when Paul says, "Put to death therefore what is earthly in you: sexual immorality, impurity, passion, evil desire, and covetousness, which is idolatry. On account of these the wrath of God is coming" (Col. 3:5-6). When we choose our own desires over God, we show that our truest heart's desire is something other than God. They expose our attempts to find more pleasure and happiness from an outside source than from Him.

We tend to believe that we can meet our own needs and find our own satisfaction through chasing the idol of pleasure. But God has not placed us here to chase pleasure. John Piper says, "God is jealous that he be honored by being treasured, and He is jealous that we be satisfied by treasuring him."[35] What does this mean? Let's revisit the marriage metaphor.

Imagine that you are married, but your spouse finds more satisfaction in another person than in you. Whether that satisfaction is emotional, intellectual, or sexual, won't her choice bring you great pain? Don't you want your spouse to commit emotionally, intellectually, and sexually to you alone? Why would God want anything different?

Paul shares that we must put to death all idols, anything that competes with our love of God. We must love God supremely, and make Him our highest affection. Our highest love. And how will we know if that's true? Our lives prove what we love.

Assess your potential idols, the things you love supremely. As you do, realize that idols might be things in your life that are good. To take it even a step further, it could even be something that God gave you for your own enjoyment. What do I mean?

I consider my own kids. I love them with such a force and such a devotion that I tend to withhold them from God. How? My daughter sometimes feels that the Lord has called her to social work in Africa. And to put it mildly, I do not want her to live overseas! Out of all of the possible futures Alex might choose, the least viable option (for me) is her moving to Africa. I can't stand the thought of Alex living on a continent thousands of miles away, one that lacks American medical care and infrastructure and is rife with government corruption. But if I love God supremely and He calls her to Africa, shouldn't I rejoice? How could I say no to God?

> *When we choose our own desires over God, we show that our truest heart's desire is something other than God.*

As you can see, even the best things can potentially be idols. My children, my wife, my music. When I'm feeling needy in general, or when I'm insecure, I tend to run to these things before I run to God. Only God can bring ultimate satisfaction, but human as we are, it's so easy to value things above God. And as understandable as it is, this is a great offense to God.

The Idolatry of Adding and Subtracting

I believe the most devious form of idolatry is when we try to add to or subtract from God's character. I say it's devious because it often happens in subtle ways. And when we do this, we're worshipping the God we want to see instead of the God who is.

God takes His name very seriously. He wants us to know who He is and what He thinks, and He wants us to walk in the truth of his Word. Therefore, when we speak or believe things about Him that are untrue, it's akin to worshipping a false God.

Let us return to an example that we have already discussed in Chapter 5. The man who claims belief in Jesus yet says that because Jesus is a God of love, He would never allow anyone to go to hell. He claims belief in Jesus but does not believe Jesus's words. The question becomes, which Jesus is being worshipped? Is it the Jesus of the Bible who claims that all of God's words are full of authority and absolute truth, or is it the Jesus that is merely defined by man's fallen idea of love?

If we create a Jesus who is solely defined by man's definition of love, then we are worshipping a God void of righteousness and justice. He is a Jesus whose words are not authoritative, not absolute, and one who could not be trusted to be faithful. Simply put, we are worshipping a different kind of God, one who is fully human but not fully divine.

When we believe things about God that are untrue, or manipulate the scriptures to read how we want them to, we are not worshipping Him as He is. Rather, we are worshipping Him as we want him to be. And these days the parts of the Bible being manipulated the most are not even the most difficult parts of the Bible to believe! For instance, the Bible would be easier to believe without the doctrine of the Trinity or the story of the virgin birth. But are these the things that most Christians struggle with today? Are these the primary arguments against the faith? Hardly. Instead, those attacking the historical faith say things like, "the Bible might be true, but I do not believe in hell or authority in marriage or authority in the church or the guidelines for sexual morality."

First, do you notice that the most common issues people currently have with the Bible are the same issues that the world is constantly obsessed with? Is it possible that our passionate feelings on these topics may be influenced by the constant messages we hear and see every single day?

To be a follower of the true Jesus means accepting Him as He is. But in our current society we see many people who claim belief in the Bible yet disbelieve some of the inconvenient truths in it. They have constructed a more convenient god. And this idol of our own creation is a god who gives us what we want and allows us to make our own judgments on morality. This god cannot not truly love us because he allows us to do whatever makes us happy without limits, just as we discussed in the previous chapter. He allows us to redefine him according to our own liking.

I have heard some people ask if it really matters if we agree on who God is as long as we are worshipping the true God. In other words, as long as we sing to Jesus, do the finer points of theology really matter? Certainly God knows our hearts and He has grace for our mistakes. And yes, of course we cannot fully and perfectly know who God is because He is infinite and we are finite. I would also agree that our understanding of God will change throughout our

To be a follower of the true Jesus means accepting Him as He is.

years of seeking Him, and these changes may include times when we realize that we had a misunderstanding of the Bible. However, there is a difference between misunderstanding God's Word and the refusal to believe His Word, and therefore, to create an idol-god of our own making.

Charles Hodge wrote, "Without right apprehensions of the Supreme Being, there can be no right affections towards him."[36] This is exactly how I felt when the girl music fan told me she loved me and cried to have her picture with me, yet she had no idea who I was. She did not love me. She loved Jacoby. In the same way, when we elevate a false view of God, we're not truly loving Him. Instead, we're loving an imposter.

THE IDOLATRY OF CULTURAL RELEVANCE

The Israelites acted no differently than we do. They constantly committed idolatry by worshipping the pagan god Baal (who was not God at all). God continued to warn them, but they continued to be unfaithful to Him. So why were they worshipping this false god?

Baal was a cultural god of the day for the nations surrounding Israel. Baal was popular. Baal was convenient. Everybody was doing it! So the Israelites would add the worship of Baal to their worship of God. This is the form of idolatry I consider most analogous to what we experience in the modern church today. We say we love Jesus. We say we need Jesus. We claim that He alone is the truth. Yet we stubbornly choose to add the gods of our culture to our worship.

How?

Consider how desperately we want to be loved. We want to be accepted. We try and find satisfaction in the approval of those around us, even in the Church! It's the reason that we no longer mention the parts of the Bible that seem offensive or old-fashioned. It's the reason our worship team members have to look a certain way or a certain age. It's why our preachers have to sound as non-antagonistic and as cool as possible. The problem with being cool is that the adoration of the world is its own kind of idol, one that robs glory from God. (Is there anything more harmful in the Church than the rise of the rock-star preacher?)

Idolatry is Adultery

Let us return now to the link between idolatry and adultery. The Bible uses extremely romantic language to express the way that God loves His people. God has made a sort of marriage covenant with His people that cannot be broken! God doesn't lie and never breaks His promises. He is a faithful God, who is not only willing but able to keep His word. And he never changes, so His covenant never changes. Incredibly, all throughout the Bible, God likens this covenant to a marriage covenant.

Consider a few passages from the Bible.

> "When I passed by you again and saw you, behold, you were at the age of love, and I spread the corner of my garment over your nakedness; I made a vow to you and entered into a covenant with you, declares the Lord God, and you became mine." (Ezek. 16:8)

> "..and as the bridegroom rejoices over the bride, so shall your God rejoice over you." (Is. 62:5)

> "I am my beloved's and my beloved is mine." (Song of Solomon 6:3)

For those who perceive God to be far off, or aloof, or a taskmaster-ing, angry disciplinarian, they are severely mistaken! The Bible speaks of a God who is passionate and zealously in love with His people. He is a God who is always patient, always kind. He never stops pursuing His glorious bride. Everyone who has been redeemed through the death of Jesus Christ is a part of His bride, and He loves His bride with an ever burning desire. And it is this covenant love that is the cause of His jealousy against our idols. He has betrothed Himself to His people. When we turn from Him and attempt to find pleasure, fulfillment, happiness, or joy in something or someone else (even our false conception of God), that is not only idolatry but it is actually committing spiritual adultery.

Of course, we are all deeply flawed, polluted by sin from the very beginning of our lives. We rebel against God at every turn because we desire to be self governed. We disbelieve His Word because we are certain that we know better! We have loved our sin. We have tried to find joy in material things rather than fulfillment in Christ. We have broken our promises to Him, and in so doing, have committed spiritual adultery by taking other lovers other than God. But do not fear! He remains steadfast to us! Praise the Lord that His covenant to us is not based on our good works nor our deeds, but rather it is based solely on His glorious grace. He has chosen us as His people, and He has made an everlasting covenant with us that cannot be broken.

If your idols are keeping you from God, tear them down. Whether those idols are some physical object, some sin that you desire more than you desire God, or some misconception of God you hold because it's more pleasant, get rid of them. God eagerly wants you to turn away from these lesser lovers and come back into the arms of your first love.

For some of us, this may require some radical move. Good! God has called His people to do radical things throughout the scriptures. Consider His call to His first love, Israel: "You shall tear down their altars and dash in pieces their pillars and burn their Asherim with fire. You shall chop down the carved images of their gods and destroy their name out of that place" (Deuteronomy 12:3).

The goodness of God is so wonderful that He will bring the fulfillment, peace, and joy that you have been searching for elsewhere. After all, He has given us what we could never earn and never deserve, an opportunity to be his bride. And this reminds me of the words of Scotty Smith, "The gospel is the story of how God makes worshipers out of idolaters, a wife out of a whore."[37] If that sounds a little harsh, it's because the truth of who we are is devastatingly brutal, yet the truth of God's faithfulness is devastatingly beautiful! So let's tear down our idols, because our jealous lover desires our all.

CHAPTER 8:
Jesus the Lion

If Jesus is loving and compassionate why does the Bible seem mean at times?

IN SIXTH grade I had thoughts I could not tell anyone. I couldn't even admit them to God, as if He didn't already know them!

The issue?

I had started reading my Bible on my own. In the version that I owned, the words that Jesus spoke during his earthly ministry were printed in red ink. My whole life I had been told that God is good. God is kind. He is close to the broken hearted. I knew Jesus was a friend of sinners. But a strange thought haunted me as I read the red letters of Jesus in the scripture. Jesus didn't sound nearly as nice to me as I had been told. But I didn't want to tell anyone because it seemed too irreverent.

As I grew a little older, I continued to hear preachers talk about how kind Jesus was to sinners. I also heard about how sinners enjoyed being with Jesus. Crowds of people followed him everywhere he went. I assumed I must be misunderstanding the Bible. And so, I stopped asking questions about the parts I didn't understand and focused on the parts I did. I read about a God who in fact was kind.

The Jesus that refused to throw a stone at a known adulterer, even though the crowd wanted to kill her for her sin.

The Jesus who visited the house of a known tax collector who cheated people out of their money.

The Jesus that taught us to pray for our enemies.

The Jesus that hung on a cross between two thieves even though he never committed a single sin, all the while asking God to forgive the very people that crucified him.

This is the Jesus that I understood. This is the Jesus that is referred to in the Bible as the Lamb of God. He is gentle, loving, and innocent as a perfect lamb headed for slaughter.

Christians are generally comfortable with the image of Jesus the lamb. However, Jesus said many things that we must reconcile with this gentle lamb imagery. He shared hard words. Serious and consequential words. He never backed down from telling the truth. Sometimes Jesus sounded less like a lamb. Sometimes he sounded more like a lion.

The more I've studied Jesus's words, the more I understand how his love necessitated the hard truths he preached. What do these hard words of Jesus teach us? First, Jesus hates pride. Second, the truth isn't always polite. Finally, radical truth requires radical words.

JESUS HATES PRIDE

Jesus's harshest criticisms were for the self-righteous, those who thought they were better than others because of their works. In self-righteousness, they couldn't see how great their need for God really was. They couldn't see that God offers His grace to all in abundance! In response, Jesus spoke harshly to the the self righteous religious people of the time.

I used to think Jesus lacked grace for these religious people because, after all, they were living under the Old Testament law. When they accused Jesus of breaking the Sabbath day of rest, for instance, they were technically correct, at least according to the letter of the law. So why did Jesus have such harsh words for them?

> *Sometimes Jesus sounded less like a lamb. Sometimes he sounded more like a lion.*

Consider Jesus's words: "But woe to you, scribes and Pharisees, hypocrites! For you shut the kingdom of heaven in people's faces. For you neither enter yourselves nor allow those who would enter to go in" (Matt. 23:13-14). What do we see in Jesus' words? God detests the proud. As James says, "God opposes the proud but gives grace to the humble" (James 4:6).

When we think that our good works and our own righteousness gain us access to God, when we preach the same to others, we earn God's wrath. This is true of all people who stand on their own works-religious or otherwise. (Remember the example from Chapter 4, the person who believes they are prepared to stand before a holy God based on their own good works?) The sad irony is that we humans are so deeply flawed and sinful that most do not even recognize how prideful this is.

The religious leaders Jesus was speaking to didn't actually love God. They did their good deeds in front of people so that they appeared to be holy. They also began to add things to the law that God did not command. It was their way of being even more "righteous" by showing God their good deeds. But by living this way, they overburdened God's people with rules and regulations that could not be kept. Instead of loving and caring for the people, they enslaved them further with needless regulations, all the while trying to use their own righteousness to domineer over them. Jesus wasn't having it.

Jesus also accused the religious teachers of leading the people astray. He called them blind guides because rather than lead the people to God, the leaders led the people into self righteous religious acts. He continued His criticism by saying that they missed the point of the law which is "justice and mercy and faithfulness"(Matt. 23:23). They wanted everyone to see them tithe and took pride in giving to God, yet they were not helping meet the needs of their people.

Jesus gets to the very heart of the matter, saying "Woe to you, scribes and Pharisees, hypocrites! For you clean the outside of the cup and the plate, but inside they are full of greed and self indulgence" (Matt. 23:25). They were clean on the outside, dirty on the inside. So, what does Jesus call them? He says they are "white washed tombs, which outwardly appear beautiful, but within are full of dead people's bones and all uncleanness" (Matt. 23:27). Due to modern language, some may not recognize how much of an insult that was. In my generation, we would call that a "pretty good burn."

Jesus shared harsh words with the self-righteous religious hypocrites. However, Jesus spoke to those in sin with a different tone. Consider the adulterous woman brought to Jesus by the religious leaders. The leaders suggested that she should be stoned to death in accordance with the Old Testament law. Jesus had compassion on the woman and answered them by saying, "Let him who is without sin among you be the first to throw a stone at her." (John 8:7). Those leaders realized it would be blaspheme to suggest they had never sinned, so they dropped their stones and left. And then, Jesus looked at this sinful woman who deserved punishment (just as we all do), and he said, "Neither do I condemn you;

go, and from now on sin no more" (John 8:11).

Here we see the stark contrast in the words of Jesus. He shared harsh truths that pierced the religious leaders' hearts, but he extended gentleness and grace to the adulterous woman. Our God is close to the broken hearted. He is a refuge and strength. He is a God who says "blessed are the poor in spirit." (Matt. 5:3).

God is gracious to us and He is a friend of sinners! But God takes great offense to the prideful self righteous soul who thinks he deserves salvation due to his own human effort. Why? Because our salvation is not about what we have done. It is about what Jesus has done.

Even though God is offended by pride, He still extends grace to us if we will turn from our sin! Notice what Jesus says to the religious leaders directly after he calls them white washed tombs in the gospel of Matthew, "O Jerusalem, Jerusalem, the city that kills the prophets and stones those who are sent to it! How often would I have gathered your children together as a hen gathers her brood under her wings, and you were not willing!" (Matt. 23:37). We see God's desire to reconcile himself to His people, even those mired in their own pride.

Truth Isn't Polite

A second reason that Jesus's words can seem harsh is because Jesus is the truth. Is the truth always easy to hear? Is the truth always nice? It depends upon your definition of nice.

Imagine I was walking along a cliff, and I didn't realize how close I was to the edge. Imagine that someone close by screamed, "hey you idiot, step away from the edge or you'll fall!" Would that be nice? I suppose there could be a more polite way to say it, but the truth is, neither he nor I would be all that concerned with politeness if my life was in danger.

And before we move on, I'll note something that is quite obvious to most older Americans but seems lost on the younger generation. Our current culture is concerned with acceptance, tolerance, inclusivity, and tone to a degree that is almost unrecognizable to previous generations. Some believe this is positive because it shows our progress to a more equitable future. But is it? Without spending much time on the subject, recognize how the extremes of inclusivity (in its social justice context) lead to banning speech that is deemed hateful or violent. Violence—under its new expanded definition—is anything that causes physical or emotional harm, distress, or offense to anyone. And since speech can be violence, we ban books and movies, and we cancel people for their past sins (judged by our current standards). We build a culture that is more concerned with tone rather than honesty, emotion rather than critical thinking, and empathy rather than truth. Jesus didn't operate this way.

Politeness is not the same thing as being kind. Jesus was in the business of telling the truth in order to save sinners from death. So though he may not have always seemed polite, he was extending the saving kindness of truth. In Matthew 19, for instance, we read the story of the rich young ruler that approached Jesus saying, "Teacher, what good deed must I do to have eternal life?" Jesus's response? He told him he must obey the commandments. The young man answered, said he'd kept every one (a certain lie). Shockingly, Jesus didn't contradict him. Instead, Jesus tells the man to sell every possession that he has, give the money to the poor, and "come, follow me." The reward? "You will have treasure in heaven," Jesus said (Matt. 19:21). Jesus words were too hard for him, and the man went away sad.

Nowhere else in scripture do we see that God calls us to sell everything that we have. Nowhere in scripture does God tell us that He wants us to live destitute lives, so why did Jesus say this? Jesus is interested in the heart. He could see past the young man's words and into the core of who he was. The man loved his money and possessions more than God, so Jesus addressed his idolatry head-on. Jesus told him the truth, though he wasn't overly polite about it! He didn't chase down the man and console him, even though his feelings were hurt. And besides, it would be unloving and insincere for Jesus to have known that the man valued possession over God and not confront him. Jesus was putting it all out on the table as if to say, "This is what it means to follow me. It will costs you everything." Saying it any other way would have meant watering down the truth, which would have been polite but ultimately unkind.

> *Jesus was in the business of telling the truth in order to save sinners from death.*

Radical Truth Requires Radical Words

The gospel of John records a story in which Jesus fed 5,000 people with only five loaves of bread and two fish. The people were awed by Jesus for this miracle and happy to have been fed, so they came back again the next day. Jesus realized that many of the people were interested in him because he fed their bodies, but he was more concerned in feeding their souls. "So, Jesus said to them, 'truly, truly, I say to you, unless you eat the flesh of the Son of man and drink his blood, you have no life in you. Whoever feeds on my flesh and drinks my blood has eternal life, and I will raise him up on the last day.' " (John 6:53-54).

Eat his flesh?

The People freaked out (understandably). This sounded like cannibalism! It was a radical notion. One that seemed to go a little too far. Maybe a lot too far. And though just ten minutes before, the people wanted this miracle teacher to be their king, now they began walking away. In fact, some of his disciples said, "This is a hard saying; who can listen to it?" (John 6:60). And many of his disciples turned back and stopped following Jesus after this.

Why didn't Jesus fix it, or explain it over again, or try a different tactic? Certainly he could have convinced some of them to stay? If only Jesus had a worship band playing emotive background music, I bet He could have won some over! But Jesus saw through to the heart of the people, and he realized that even though they were following him, they did not actually believe in him. He didn't soften his message because...wait for it.. he actually believed in his message! It was not enough to accept his miracles. The people had to believe and partake of him. And that's still the truth today.

Jesus shares radical words relating to sin and hell, too. The Jesus that loves sinners and had compassion for the adulterous woman is also the Jesus that hates sin. In his Sermon on the Mount, he wrote, "If your right eye makes you to sin, tear it out and throw it away. For it is better that you lose one of your members than that   your whole body to be thrown into hell" (Matt. 5:29-30). Jesus went on to say the very same thing about your hand—if it causes you to sin, it should be better to cut it off than to have your whole body thrown into hell.

"Too far!" some may say. And though it may seem extreme, Jesus didn't say anything unless the Father told him to. These are the words of God! And through these words, he's showing us a radical truth: Though the physical is temporary, the spiritual is eternal. It is not our bodies that ultimately matter, it is our souls.

Jesus shares hard words regarding anger, too. In the Old Testament, God forbids murder. In the New Testament, Jesus raised the bar. He taught that not only shall we not murder, "But I say to you that everyone who is angry with his brother will be liable to judgment; whoever insults his brother will be liable to the council; and whoever says, 'you fool!' Will be liable to the hell of fire" (Matt. 5:22). We are not even allowed to be angry with our brother? Talk about a hard teaching!

In our modern churches we shy away from the harshness of the reality of sin, and we tend to focus more on the fact that Jesus understands our pain and forgives our sin. It is indeed wonderful news that Jesus understands and forgives! However, the more we soften his words about his hatred for sin—including anger—the less we understand our depravity and the state of our sin. Furthermore, if we do not vividly understand the consequences of our sin, the we will not understand how much we desperately need to be forgiven! This is why Jesus desires to convey through his words the degree in which we are polluted by sin. He wants us to understand that we are without any hope of ever earning righteousness on our own. He wants us to understand just how desperately we need to partake in him. Without the Spirit of God changing us from the inside out, we have no hope of cleansing ourselves from sin. And if we don't receive pardon from our sin, there are consequences. And this brings us to, perhaps, Jesus's most fearsome and radical teaching.

Many Christians and church leaders do not believe that God would allow anyone to go to hell. "God is love," they argue, "and he loves all his creation, so how could he torment it in an eternal hell?" However, not only does the Bible talk about hell and eternal punishment, but the hardest, most shocking things said about hell were said by Jesus himself! If you don't believe me then read the red letters.

As we have already seen, Jesus said if someone calls a brother a fool then he is labile to hell. Jesus said if someone's eye or hand causes them to sin, it's better to pluck out the eye or cut off the hand than for us to be cast into hell. What does Jesus say about the ones who never followed him? He said, "'Depart from me, you cursed, into the eternal fire prepared for the devil and his angels'" (Matt. 25:41). Jesus was not shy about his thoughts concerning wickedness and the wicked. And yes, they are radical.

Without these radical words, we would not have known the truth of our sin and its consequences. Sin kills. Sin hurts. Sin is slavery. God wants to free you from sin and raise you to new life, both in this world and in the life to come.

Cost of Following

In America, we tend to beg people to follow Christ. We even make it as easy as possible. We don't offend, and we certainly don't tell all of the truth, lest people may not want to follow! Jesus was not nearly as bashful.

A man came to Jesus and said he would follow Jesus no matter where he went. Jesus answered, "Foxes have holes and birds of the air have nests, but the Son of Man has nowhere to lay his head" (Luke 9:58). The Scriptures do not indicate whether the man followed, but because it doesn't expressly say he did, we can infer that the man turned away.

On another occasion, Jesus invited a man to come and follow him, to which the man responded, "Lord, let me first go and bury my father" (Luke 9:59). That seems reasonable doesn't it? Jesus's response? "Leave the dead to bury their own dead. But as for you, go, and proclaim the kingdom of God" (Luke 9:60). Now that is insensitive! Still, it was loving because Jesus knew that some will always make excuses for not following Jesus immediately. As the gospel-writer Luke records, "If anyone would come after me, let him deny himself and take up his cross daily and follow me" (Luke 9:23).

> ...because Jesus loved us perfectly, we must hear his words as if spoken by a father, one who wants to save us from the worst punishment.

The gospel of Jesus Christ is one of life-altering and radical change. It is only logical that Jesus's teachings would be radical. He knew that whomever follows radically, whomever loses their life for Christ's sake would be given life more abundantly, both now and forever. And because Jesus loved us perfectly, we must hear his words as if spoken by a father, one who wants to save us from the worst punishment.

So, let's not create a new god who only speaks words that we deem polite and permissible and does not offend our ideas of tolerance. May we praise God for all of His words, even the hard ones! Let us continue to love Jesus as a friend, but not forget to bow down before Him as the King of Kings, as the lion and as the lamb.

CHAPTER 9:
Shock and Awe

What's in it for me?

Throughout this book, we've mostly considered the truth of sin and the brokenness of human reasoning. So, let's turn to triumph, particularly the triumph written about in the Scriptures! If we are to trust the Bible as the absolute authority of God, then we must be prepared to believe some absolutely amazing truths about His goodness to us!

When I was growing up I was extremely hyperactive, which may come as no surprise for those of you who've seen *Skillet* in concert. I've always had tons of energy, so much that it's sometimes annoying to those around me. And though I was not a malicious kid, I got in trouble constantly, mostly due to my energetic and oblivious nature.

When I was very young, maybe five-years old, I had some kind of energetic outburst, the kind that landed me in deep trouble with my parents. I don't remember what I did, but I'll never forget my mom's reaction. She sat me on her bed and explained how she would never stop loving me, even when she was mad. I was shocked and could barely believe it. "Really?" I said, and to this day I recall her laughing as she said "of course silly! Nothing could ever stop me from loving you because I'm your mom."

It's interesting how we remember certain moments in our lives that were shaping or life-altering. This was one for me. And many of you have had similar conversations with your own parents, or even with your kids. And though the thought of unconditional love from a parent is obvious now, it was earth shattering for little five-year old John.

It was the first time I made an intellectual connection with the concept of love that is not earned. It is easy to love people who love you or are good to you. It is easy to repay kindness with kindness. But to repay wickedness with kindness is something altogether different. It makes sense when a parent loves you because you make good grades and clean up your room. But parents who love you when you are in rebellion against them, purposely disobey them, and tell them that you hate them is a much bigger testament to love.

We have spent many chapters examining how each of us has acted towards God. Like the children who live in rebellion and hate their parents, we treat His commands as optional and turn our affections to other things. Now, prepare to be shocked at the amazing truth of the way God lavishes His love upon us. For those who have been redeemed in Christ Jesus, not only do we not receive the punishment we deserve, but instead, He gives us grace, forgiveness, family, righteousness, and royalty! We are like the adulterous bride who returns home, not to find an angry husband, but to be embraced by a husband who prepares a feast in celebration of our return.

Heirs of the Promise

Faithfulness is in short supply these days. We make a marriage vow "until death do us part." That is a covenant promise of love, and still, nearly half of all marriages end in divorce. Why? Because human faithfulness is fickle. Perhaps we fall out of love with our spouse. Perhaps one has an affair and is sexually unfaithful. In fact, upon looking into the Bible on a deeper level, we read that if someone even looks at another person (who is not your spouse) with lust in their heart, then that person is guilty of unfaithfulness. In other words, faithfulness to a human is at best still tainted by our own desires.

To God, faithfulness is something entirely different. God is faithful in the true sense of the term. Meaning, He never fails. Ever. He does not grow tired of keeping His promise. He never grows bored. He never changes. He cannot lie. In other words, whatever he says He will do, He will absolutely do! Consider the words recorded in Deuteronomy: "Know therefore that the Lord your God is God, the faithful God who keeps covenant and steadfast love with those who love him and keep his commandments, to a thousand generations." (Deut. 7:9).

So what has He promised?

First, let's recall that because of Adam's sin and how it has polluted the entirety of the human race, we are born spiritually dead. The holiness of God demands that sin be cast away from His presence. But there is great news! God has made way for us to have life now and for all eternity! He has promised that in Him, we will never die. In Him, we will never age. In Him, we will never again suffer! And He can make these promises because of His absolute faithfulness, even to the death.

Jesus was so faithful, that he took the penalty of our sin on himself. When Jesus died on the cross, our sin was placed on Him. He knew it would cost him his life, and still, he continued to the cross in absolute faithfulness. And when we have faith in the work that Jesus did for us on the cross, God gives us a brand new heart. Whereas we once had a sin-filled heart of stone that was lifeless, the Bible says Christ gives us a living heart of flesh. Why? Because in His faithfulness, all of the pollution of sin that was caused by Adam's sin is now forgiven. As a result, we can live in eternity with God.

But not only have we been given life for all eternity, we have a foretaste of that life while we are here on earth. We experience that life abundantly in the fact that God has now made a home for Himself in our hearts. Yes, the Spirit of God lives inside of those who believe in Him! He gives us faith. He encourages us to walk in God's ways and gives us the power to fulfill that calling.

What's more, he puts the kingdom inside of us. And what does it mean to have the kingdom living in us? The Bible says "...the kingdom of God is not a matter of eating and drinking but of righteousness and peace and joy in the Holy Spirit" (Rom. 14:17). While the world experiences chaos, we have peace and order. While the world experiences hopelessness, we experience joy. Even when devastation hits and our lives are thrown upside down, and even when we cannot laugh because the pain is too great, we will endure! We still have joy to hold on to. When our loved ones die, when our children are sick or suffering, when we lose our jobs, we find ultimate peace and joy in the never-changing faithful promise of God-given abundant life!

A Brief History of God's Faithfulness

The faithfulness of God goes on forever. But to understand how God's faithfulness has played out over history we must look back to the earthly father of our faith in the Old Testament, Abraham. In the book of Genesis, God told Abraham, "...I will establish my covenant between me and you and your offspring after you throughout their generations for an everlasting covenant, to be God to you and to your offspring after you" (Gen. 17:7). God established an unbreakable promise with Abraham to give him and his descendants life and blessing and to be their faithful God. In the New Testament we read that Abraham had faith in God, and God counted it to him as righteousness. And as God's plan of redemption unfolded, the Bible demonstrates how the true children of Abraham are those who have faith in God. Abraham's true children are not natural born descendants, but rather, they are spiritually born. As Paul wrote to the church in Romans, "...It is not the children of the flesh who are the children of God, but the children of promise are counted as offspring" (Rom. 9:8). Therefore all of the promises that God made to Abraham and his children are for us, so long as we believe in his Truth!

This is why the Bible calls us "heirs according to of promise" (Gal. 3:29). But what are the amazing promises? God promises He will be our God, and we will be his people (Jer. 30:22). He says that He will bless us (Deut. 30:3), protect us (Deut. 31:6), care for us as a father (Deut. 32:6), and love us like a faithful husband (Is. 54:5). Finally, God promises that we will be resurrected to new life eternal. Jesus said, "And as for the resurrection of the dead, have you not read what was said to you by God: 'I am the God of Abraham, and the God of Isaac, and the God of Jacob'? He is not God of the dead, but of the living" (Matt. 22:31). John Piper writes concerning this passage,

> Therefore, God's justification of Abraham by faith is full of promise: it means he is forgiven and freed from condemnation, and that God is his God and will work for him to bless him in this age and give him eternal life in the age to come.[38]

God promises us life! We are the children of the promise that God gave to Abraham, and God never breaks His promises. We will have life for eternity, and a foretaste of that life now. We experience a taste of the benefits of the Kingdom of God here and now. However, the good news doesn't stop here!

WE HAVE BEEN SET FREE!

If sin leads to death and we are born into the slavery of sin, then how can we stop serving our sinful desires? How can we be free? This is part of God's promise to give us life abundantly. He breaks the power of sin over us! In fact, this is our only hope to fight sin.

If we're honest, each of us has a desire for sin and its pleasures. However, the passing pleasure of sin soon leaves us dissatisfied and frustrated. Sin cannot fully satisfy, so we try and fill ourselves up with even more sin. All the while, our hearts become harder to the Spirit of God. And often, we don't even realize that we are in a vicious sin cycle!

Most desire to be free from sin and to be made whole, even if we can't articulate it. This is part of the sorrow we experience as a result of Adam's fall. But for the Christian, there is freedom and wholeness. There is life! It is found in the chain-breaking power of Christ! The Bible says "For freedom Christ has set us free; stand firm therefore, and do not submit again to a yoke of slavery!" (Gal. 5:1).

Too many Christians do not understand the amazing power of God at work in their lives. The Spirit of God is powerful enough to break addictions! He can break bad habits, help us control our tongues, and even help us rule over our evil thoughts. We do not have to wait until we get to heaven to enjoy victory over sin. It is true that we do not walk in a *fullness* of victory yet (after all, we're still walking around in broken bodies). However, our victory against sin begins now! As Paul wrote, "We know that our old self was crucified with him in order that the body of sin might be brought to nothing, so that we would no longer be enslaved to sin." (Rom. 6:6). God has set you free! Even if you don't feel free, if you are a believer in Christ, you are! Will we believe His word over our feelings?

> *Even if you don't feel free, if you are a believer in Christ, you are! Will we believe His word over our feelings?*

Even though the power of sin is broken over us, even though we are free, we will still wrestle against sin as long as we are in these earthly bodies. The strength to fight our own sinful desires is not found in our own will power, but in God's faithfulness that can bring us to a place where we are able to fight sin, not in our own strength, but rather in His strength.

Notice the words of Paul when he was struggling with his own affliction. He wrote,

> Three times I pleaded with the Lord about this, that it should leave me. But he said to me, 'My grace is suffi-

cient for you, for my power is made perfect in weakness.'
Therefore I will boast all then more gladly of my weaknesses, so that then power of Christ may rest upon me.
(2 Cor. 12:8-9)

Whether Paul was struggling with sickness or sin, we may never know. Here's what we do know: He overcame through the power of Christ.

God's promise to us is not that we will never again be tempted by sin. His promise is that He has set us free from it's power, and He will help us win the fight against the flesh. If you are struggling with sin and it is causing you to disbelieve that God has broken its power over you, then it's time to trust in the words of God. He never lies!

FORGIVEN AND RECREATED

Some Christians struggle with guilt over their past sins. Other Christians struggle with guilt over their current sins and struggles. And the truth is, many people who aren't Christians struggle with guilt and shame, too. I can relate to this. Can you? After all, our sins leave us empty. What's more, they make us unclean before God. How can it be remedied?

God promises us that He will forgive and erase our sins if we place our trust in Him. He washes us whiter than snow. First, concerning forgiveness the Bible says, "As far as the east is from the west, so far does he remove our transgressions from us" (Psalm 103:12). God keeps no record of our wrongs. We stand before Him just as if we had never sinned. Ever. Not one single hint of sin!

God's forgiveness is so complete that it gives us safety and security from His wrath. I meet many people who say that they struggle with believing that God has truly forgiven them. I think this is because we are so terrible at forgiving others. We are bad at forgiveness. We desire to be forgiven, of course, yet we hardly ever offer full forgiveness to others. Even for petty violations. The person who cuts us off in traffic. The spouse who is short tempered simply because he or she had a bad day. Don't even get me started about the Starbucks employee who botches our order. But God does not forgive like we do. His forgiveness is complete and absolute.

To demonstrate the depths of God's love, notice the severity of His hatred against sin. The wrath of God is mentioned over 500 times in the Old Testament, always toward the sin of his people. He will not allow even a hint of sin in His presence. But Jesus bore every last drop of our iniquity, and as a result, became the object of God's wrath for our sin.

Of Jesus's sacrifice, the Gospel writer John put it this way: "He is the propitiation for our sins, and not for ours only but also for the sins of the whole world" (1 John 2:2). "Propitiation" means an appeasement for wrath. So, if you believe in Christ, then God has absolutely no wrath against your sin any longer. The debt has been paid, His wrath has been satisfied, and you are totally and completely forgiven! This is why John could write, "If we confess our sins, he is faithful and just to forgive us our sins and to cleanse us from all unrighteousness" (1 John 1:9).

But wait, there's more! God doesn't just forgive us, but He recreates us entirely. Notice that there is a difference between forgiveness and recreation. Forgiveness is wiping the slate clean. But God's goodness towards us does not stop simply with a righting of wrongs. He actually makes us a new creation (2 Cor. 5:17). He changes us from the inside out, making us what we could never have been without Him.

The Bible says that God gives us a divine nature. And this doesn't just insinuate a "better" nature, or merely a "supernatural" nature. It denotes the divine nature. Meaning, the very nature of God lives inside of us now! Hear the glorious words of Paul to the Ephesians: "And to put on the new self, created after the likeness of God in true righteousness and holiness" (Eph 4:24). Also listen to the words of Paul to the Corinthians: "For our sake he made him to be sin who knew no sin, so that in him we might become the righteousness of God" (2 Cor. 5:21). About this latter passage, the Bible scholar Charles J. Ellicott writes, "The importance of the passage does in its presenting the truth that the purpose of God in the death of Christ was not only or chiefly that men might escape punishment, but that they might become righteous."[39]

God's promise to you concerning forgiveness and recreation is amazing. Because of Jesus's work on the cross, we now share in His very nature. And after we die we will see Him face to face, and we will be completely transformed and will be made like Him.

Sons and Daughters of Glory

As incredible as it seems, because we are partakers of the divine nature, we are truly adopted sons and daughters of God. This means that we are siblings of our Lord, Jesus Christ Himself. What's more, "and if children, then heirs- heirs of God and fellow heirs with Christ provided we suffer with him in order that we may also be glorified with him." (Rom. 8:17).

God loves each of His children with same love that He has for His own glorious Son. He loves us so much that he wants to glorify us with Christ! Could we even make this up? It is too good to fathom!

Not only are we co-heirs with Christ, but we are also one with Him. Paul wrote, "For you have died, and your life is hidden with Christ in God" (Col. 3:3). This language so closely ties us together with Jesus, our co-heir, the Bible says we "are the body of Christ" (1 Cor. 12:27). We are not literally his physical features, of course. But we are joined and inseparable from Him. Therefore, as we stand before God the Father, we are blameless in His sight! When God the Father sees you, He sees His son!

In Chapter 3 we briefly discussed the fact that God loves and enjoys Himself. He speaks love and joy and ultimate satisfaction to Himself because He is perfect and glorious. We know that the Father is pleased with Jesus, and He dearly loves the Son. The love and joy that God has for Himself is the same love and joy that he has for you and me for all eternity-because when the Father sees us, we are hidden in Christ. We will be wearing the righteousness of Jesus like a robe of glory! Is there any safer place to be than hidden in the righteousness of Christ?

Awestruck

God makes us promises that He cannot and will not break. If you are suffering from depression, you are not alone because He is with you. If you are struggling with patterns of sin or addiction, you can know that Christ has set you free from its power! If you are weak in the fight against sin, He promises that He will be strong through you. If you do not have an earthly father, God

> *God makes us promises that He cannot and will not break.*

the Father loves you with the same measure He loves his Son. If you are poor, God has made you rich by giving you the greatest treasure, which is the gift of Himself! If you are the outcast who is rejected, God has called you His family.

If we woke up every day and took a moment to remind ourselves of the truth, our lives would be different. If we opened our eyes each morning and said, "it is time for one of the sons of God to get out of bed, clothed in the righteousness of Christ, and be led by the Holy Spirit to bring Kingdom rule and dominion to the world around me, starting with my own flesh" what might happen? My guess? We'd live more fulfilled, more Kingdom-oriented, more world-changing lives. The result? Our hearts would be overflowing with joy from the pleasure we would find in the Father.

CHAPTER 10:
Life or death

So what should I do now?

The only time in my life where I struggled with doubt (for more than a few hours, anyway) was my first week of college. I was totally unprepared for the battle ahead of me. In fact, I was unaware there even was a battle.

The first day of college I was bombarded in three different classrooms by atheist professors. By the end of the first day, I carried these lessons back to my room: only fools believe in any god of any sort; science is the only truth; the Bible is full of fairy tales; the Bible contradicts itself; only superstitious rednecks and uneducated people believe in Christianity; and you'll never be taken seriously as an academic if you believe in the Bible. For the first time in my life I wondered if I had been fed lies. I felt the professors laughing at me.

To make matters worse, college opened up new opportunities for sin and pleasure, opportunities I hadn't had before. At college orientation, I met a few people and as we were walking to the nighttime gathering some guy said, "I hope this isn't one of those stupid male-bonding activities." The girl walking next to me (who I had just met and I didn't even catch her name) looked at me and said, "Me too, but I'd be up for some sexual bonding. How about you?" I was too shocked to even respond, but when I could gather my words, I politely declined. A few days later during the second day of classes, I was in line at the cafeteria, waiting to check out when I felt something hot and wet on the back of my neck. I sort of jumped and twisted around, and a girl I'd never seen said "I'm sorry, but c'mon, you've got a nibble neck."

The pressure was mounting. My mom died and I don't understand why God would allow it— how could I believe God was good? And there I was in college, denying myself all sorts of worldly pleasures in order to live in accordance with my faith. What's more, my professors were telling me my faith was a joke, a lie, something uneducated people believe because they do not understand basic science. And in the light of those pressures, I was forced to ask the question: Is living for Jesus really worth it?

During that first week of college, I prayed. I talked to my pastor. I asked God to make Himself known to me. God had been faithful to me all these years. He had never failed me. Not once. So, I opened my Bible, and over the next three days I read. And read. And read some more. Then one afternoon between classes I read this, from the apostle Paul: "But God chose what is foolish in the world to shame the wise; God chose what is weak in the world to shame the strong." (1 Cor. 1:27).

That's it!

I remembered the truth. Though I may seem foolish, it's the one who says "there is no God" that is the actual fool. (Psalm 14:1). And this is why the arrogant are so miserable. They may be intelligent, but they lack true wisdom, which begins with the fear of the Lord. (Proverbs 9:10).

During that week, my eyes were open to the battle ahead. And if I had not opened up the Bible and trusted God's Word, my life would have turned out very differently. I wouldn't have met Korey, and we wouldn't have had Alex and Xavier. I wouldn't have started the band Skillet. Even more, I wouldn't have had the true peace and joy of Christ. But thanks to the grace of God, I am enjoying the benefits of trusting and obeying the words of Jesus.

So now, let us return to the beginning, to where we started in Chapter 1. Let's return to the words of Jesus about the man who built his house on the sand and the one who built his house on the rock. We have a choice to make. We are presented with two radical options in our pursuit of truth. We can either build on the sand of our own emotions, or we can trust in God. One leads to death. The latter leads to life.

OPTION 1: TRUSTING IN SELF

We can choose to trust ourselves. We can follow our own inner guide. But as I've argued, ultimate truth is hidden from us because we are fallen beings. And not only do we not recognize the truth but we also actively wage war against it. We follow our extreme hunger for power and greed and selfishness. We follow our own desire for autonomy, which rebels against true righteousness because we want to supplant God and sit on His throne.

Maybe you do not agree with my assessment. But let me ask you—how will you aim to find truth? Will you will follow your heart, do what you feel to be right? Will you follow your inner voice? But what will you do when your heart changes? Will your truth change, too?

By visiting our youth, we can see just how easy it is for our hearts to change. When I was a child I wanted to be Spider-man. Until I wanted to be Batman. And shortly after that, I was sure I was going to be a professional basketball player (until I found out that I was terrible at the sport). In my teen years I met a dozen girls that I was sure I wanted to be with forever. Then, overnight, I couldn't stand to be around them anymore. And yes, these are mostly light hearted examples, but the truth is, most of us have experienced the ways the heart leads us astray.

Need more serious examples?

How many marriages end in divorce because each was following their heart? How many people are unfaithful to their spouse based on a sexual escapade that just felt right at the time? How many addictions do we justify because we love the way it feels? And these are just the more extreme versions. How many of us have had buyers remorse over a car, house, or television? How many have regretted moving to a city they thought they'd love or taking a job they were sure would make them happy? How many have regretted their first tattoo?

The heart is wicked and deceitful. And from a philosophical point of view, how could such finite, insignificant beings know the absolute truth of the world simply by following their hearts? If the heart can lead you to get an ugly tattoo in your youth, then certainly the heart can lead you into destruction.

Furthermore, is it virtuous to follow our hearts when our desires destroy other people? A man follows his heart into the arms of another lover, in the meantime destroying his marriage and his children. Following their hearts, humans have enslaved others for their own economic prosperity. Every dictator in history believed in the moral superiority of their own actions, even while slaughtering the most vulnerable under their rule.

Perhaps you know you can't trust your own heart, and so, you take your truth-cues from society. To some degree, this makes logical sense. Conforming to society's truth helps you assimilate keeps you from running afoul of the law. But in another sense, society tells you how to live according to the subjective truth of the day. So let me ask: how is that working out for society these days? Is it going well? Or does the world outside your window feel as if it's falling into chaos?

An ever changing system of morality defined by academic elites, politicians, media, or social-media social justice warriors is, by definition, a house built on the sand. Rules are made. Rules are changed. Rules are even broken. And if this isn't enough, consider the ways that even our language has changed in the last few years. During interviews or at speaking events, I find myself forced to use lengthy sentences to explain what I mean when only five years ago I could have just used one word that would efficiently and concisely relay my thoughts. Why is this? Because our very language no longer holds objective meaning.

It may seem silly, but consider the amount of words that no one intends to be negative but which have suddenly become offensive—man up, pyscho, thug, lame, and rioting (just to list a few). These petty offenses can cost you an apology at work or cause you to lose a friend at a PTA meeting or put you in Twitter jail. And if the lack of intent or lack of knowledge of the "new definition" is mentioned, the offense is even worse. It almost seems that being unaware of the new moral standard is an entirely unforgivable infraction on its own. How does someone stay in good graces?

> *An ever changing system of morality defined by academic elites, politicians, media, or social-media social justice warriors is, by definition, a house built on the sand.*

On a more serious note, it's not just language that's being torn down. One day the "powers that be" elevate a particular person, the next day they cancel the same person. They jockey for position at the top of the progressive pyramid. And then, someone reaches up and pulls the person at the top down. Issues gives way to issue, too. Protests gives way to protest, each aiming to tear down some structure. The result? A society that is absolutely exhausted.

My generation—Generation X—glamorized hedonism, or chasing our own desires. Modern culture glamorizes humanism instead, the idea that we are the center of our universe and the answer to all our problems. I believe that this modern shift to humanism leads to more frustration than a life of hedonism. Oddly, this seems to put me in the awkward position of defending hedonism, which I abhor, but indulge me for a moment.

The person who simply lives for pleasure will ultimately be dissatisfied from the temporal nature of pleasure. However, it should be noted that the hedonist does not consider their pursuit of pleasure to be virtuous. Their disillusionment is found only in the fact that self gratification isn't all that gratifying. The modern social justice warrior, on the other hand, is disillusioned on two levels. First, the gratification of being in the right crowd is short-lived. Second, there is no lasting joy in self-righteousness, especially when the rules change and the Twitter mob comes calling.

Let's be honest. The self-righteousness of humanism is not only repulsive to those around us, but it's also the emptiest of all vices. In other vices we are under the illusion that we are happy. In self-righteousness we convince ourselves that we are good.

OPTION 2: TRUSTING IN GOD

The second option to finding truth is just as radical. It flows from the belief that God wants to bring redemption to mankind, that He wants to restore His image in us. He wants to give us what we could never find and never earn on our own! He wants to make us sons and daughters and let us share in His glory. The question now becomes, will we have the audacity to believe in these amazing words of God? Could we dare to believe something so radical?

Trusting in God requires a radical response because it is radical truth. I recall the school shooting at Columbine High School where Cassie Bernall was killed. She had a gun pointed at her head and the shooter asked her a simple question, "Do you believe in God?" Cassie famously answered "yes," knowing that she likely would be martyred because of that acknowledgment. Do you think that she regrets that answer now that she is face to face with the Lord Jesus Christ? Absolutely not! She confessed her Savior before men, knowing that Jesus will acknowledge her before God the Father. There is a reason that people die for their faith in Christ, even in the modern age. Their hearts have been captured by something that is more valuable to them than their life. And if it was true that God can do all of the things I have mentioned, would it be worth giving up your life for it? Would anyone disagree that life for eternity is far more important than our limited number of years on earth?

I cannot convince you that the Bible is real, of course. But imagine for a moment that it is. Would you agree that the radical words of the Bible are better than money, riches, fame, or earthly pleasure? Certainly, the riches that come from God—both in this life and in the life to come—are incomparably better than being a YouTube sensation, or in my case, in a well-known rock band.

You cannot weigh earthly pleasure against eternal pleasure. Eternal pleasure has no end. It cannot be measured. One of the reasons earthly pleasure passes so quickly is because we humans are not created with the capacity to enjoy constant pleasure. We get tired, we get full, we get bored. We get tired of eating the same old thing at our favorite restaurant, so we eat something else until we tire of that. We listen to our favorite album until we grow bored with it, then we find a new band. We might cycle through women, substances, or social media feeds until we need a new fix. This is the simple truth of human appetites. They do not satisfy us.

Our bodies cannot enjoy endless pleasure because we are finite. But God offers us life for eternity in a new body that is fit to be tirelessly and perfectly satisfied and joyful! This is why those who follow God are willing to sacrifice all for Him. He is our joy forevermore! Whether you call it zeal, passion, or even obsession, the follower of Christ has a burning desire like fire in our bones. And if you don't have that same fire, there's only one question remaining: Will you believe?

Fun is not Fulfillment

I have met a great many people in the the music business who seem to be happy. They have money and fame and celebrity, which is arguably what the world covets most. Many are not joyful, though, and they wouldn't make such a claim. After all, it's hard to have joy when you are in slavery to addiction, whether to chemical substances, alcohol, fame, or the praise of men. And while it may be fun at times, all of it leads to soul dissatisfaction.

If given the option, I believe most people would prefer to be fulfilled than to have fun, including those I mentioned above. It might be fun to record music, to travel the world with a band, to be recognized on the street, but it's not ultimately fulfilling. In fact, the very thing that is fun becomes extremely unfulfilling, particularly as any sort of difficulty sets in. But as I've experienced, fulfillment is possible, though only through God who wants to satisfy our souls. When we are satisfied and fulfilled in Him, we will not long for temporary fun. We will not be satisfied with earthly pleasure. He will be more pleasurable than anything else.

When we build our houses on fun, pleasure, or anything other than

God, it always leaves us unfulfilled. Why? Consider Solomon, the wisest, wealthiest man who ever lived. He was the king, had women at his beck and call, and experienced all of the world's greatest pleasures. He sought pleasure in both work and leisure. He sought pleasure in his intellect. But chasing all these pleasures left him empty.

Solomon recorded his experience in the book of Ecclesiastes. He wrote that everything is utterly meaninglessness. He says "What does man gain by all the toil at which he toils under the sun?"(Eccles. 1:3). Nothing lasts. Nothing brings soul satisfaction. When we're not satisfied, we tend to believe it is because we have not experienced enough pleasure. We'll chase more money, more fame, more alcohol, more whatever. But no matter how much of anything we consume, it will never be enough. Solomon assures us of this truth. In fact, he assures us the pursuit of it all left him empty and in despair. (Ecclesiastes 2:20).

This is profound, but think about this—Solomon shows us that it is not the *rich* man who is ultimately the most unsatisfied but rather it is the *richest* man who suffers the most due to life's disillusionments. It is the richest man who has fully uncovered all that there is to uncover. There is nowhere else to go, nowhere else to climb, and no hope for another discovery that will bring satisfaction. There are no more wells to drink from and every one of them leaves him with the same unquenched thirst. We see this truth in the famous quote attributed to Alexander the Great, "When Alexander saw the breadth of his domain, he wept for there were no more worlds to conquer."

Discovering the Truth Brings Fulfillment

I heard a true story from a friend about a man who had created several businesses, had many employees, and created an incredible amount of wealth. He'd never be in need of anything that he couldn't buy. There was nothing left to conquer because he had reached the top of the mountain of success. In his later years in life he discovered the truth of Jesus and the God of the universe. He had finally found the joy and fulfillment he had been looking for in all of his endless pursuits. He was asked what he wanted to do for the remaining years of his life. His answer was simple:

In the time I have left, as I climb down the mountain of

success and pass everyone who is clawing and scraping their way up, I want to tell them as loudly as I can that I have been to the top of the mountain. I have seen everything there is to see. And there is nothing up there.

God has an answer for us to find fulfillment and meaning. That feeling in your heart that tells you there must be more to life, that we must be here for a reason, that there is a greater destiny—these universal instincts are placed in the hearts of men and women by God. We know that something is very wrong, but we just don't know how to fix it. God tells us through the words of Solomon that everything we pursue in this life as an ultimate thing is meaningless and empty, because we are not ultimately created for this life. We were created for eternity.

> *That feeling in your heart that tells you there must be more to life, that we must be here for a reason, that there is a greater destiny—these universal instincts are placed in the hearts of men and women by God.*

If Solomon says that everything under the sun is meaningless, then we must search for something that is beyond the sun! We'll never find truth in ourselves, our own feelings, or our own pursuits. We are not equipped for it. It is impossible. As we have seen, it is also folly to trust a society that doesn't believe in truth. Not only does it lead to chaos, but Solomon also shows us that trusting in ourselves is unfulfilling.

If you do not believe Solomon, then perhaps you will believe a modern celebrity. How many rich and beautiful celebrities have died in the last decade due to suicide or accidental overdose? Many musical greats have met this end—such as Michael Jackson, Prince, Chester Bennington, just to name a few. And many who don't die finally check into rehab facilities, and when they emerge, they share their stories. Addiction was slavery. Though it was pleasurable for a while, the joy of being free far outweighs the temporal pleasures of soul slavery. And for every celebrity who says that about drugs, alcohol, or sex addiction, you'll find just as many who say that about fame and fortune.

The Best is yet to Come

More than a few of you may read this and make arguments against trusting God. You might say that trusting God is illogical. Okay. I hear you. But our trust in God is not based on pure logic, but on faith! Still, this does not mean that trusting God is illogical. Far from it! What's more, I believe it is illogical to attempt to find absolute truth on your own.

Believing you are capable of unlocking all of the eternal truths and secrets of the ages, all by using the knowledge contained within your own head seems like madness. I cannot even solve a Rubik's Cube! And witnessing a society that cannot balance their own checkbooks, that is experiencing an epidemic of mass suicide along with unprecedented rates of anxiety and mental health issues, that is spiraling into chaos—does that give me hope that humans can unravel the mysteries of the universe? They can't even unravel the mysteries of maintaining an ordered society! I contend that it is more logical to believe in the existence of God than to to believe that humans can offer better solutions than Him.

Another argument made against trusting God is that God is too demanding, too violent, or too mean. "He doesn't want us to have any fun!" they say. The truth is that God wants you to be free much more than He wants you to have fun. You may not be aware of your own soul slavery, and you might even believe you are on a pathway to ultimate fulfillment. More money, a more fulfilling job, a better marriage, perfect children, more influence on political legislation, or more opportunities to make a difference. But what happens if you eventually reach your goal and get to the top of the mountain, only to find that there is nothing up there? What if you wake up to find that you are living your life much like the humans in their pods in The Matrix. You are a slave to the problems of this world—chained to your job, to your desires, and ultimately to sin. And all the while, you thought so much of it was fun.

God wants to set you free. It's not because He doesn't want you to have fun. He knows that when you taste of His goodness, it will be more pleasurable to you than everything else! God wants you to turn away from your lesser lovers, abandon your idols, and find your greatest fulfillment in Him!

Choose the ultimate truth, and become a child of the promise. How? Just ask God to show you the truth in His Word and believe in Him. Open your eyes to your need of forgiveness. Repent of your own brokenness and sin, turn to

God, and be ready to be amazed at the overwhelming perfect love of God. It can start right here, right now. Whether you are at work, at school, at lunch, or alone in your room as I was. Wherever you are, God is there with you. And if you do not know what to say, just begin with this childlike statement: *Jesus, I give my heart to you, and you are the boss.* Come awake. Come alive. Then, see what happens. See if you don't notice something like joy, peace, and ultimate fulfillment setting in, both today, and for the journey ahead.

ACKNOWLEDGEMENTS

Thank you to Jesus who is the Truth. To Korey—without you I would be virtually unrecognizable. You are not only the "better half", you are the only good half. Alex, and Xavier—I have no words to describe what you mean to me so I will not even try. You bring me more joy than I deserve. To Zach Kelm (manager) and Velvet Kelm (publicist), WOW its been 20 years together and I couldn't have done it without you. To Zach, I will simply say this, "Frodo wouldn't have gotten very far without Sam." To Jennifer Fleming and Sarah Scales and the great many people who have worked alongside at Q Management I want to say sincerely, thank you for everything. To my editor, Seth Haines, you are a Godsend and a necessity. To my extended Skillet family—Jen ledger, Seth Morrison, and all of my wonderful crew—its been an honor. My attorney, Todd Rubenstein; Jeff Roberts and associates, Josh Humiston and my friends at APA; Breanne and everyone at Martin, Albee, Miller, Bryan, & Associates; Andy Karp, Pete Ganbarg, and the amazing Lea Piscane, and all my faithful friends and partners at Atlantic Records; Word records, and so many others in the business at radio I say thank you for years of support. Josh Frankel at Z2 comics! My wonderful church family who has been foundational in our lives, our extended natural families, so many friends and fellow workers in the faith, way too many people to mention that were influential along the way—thanks for your faithfulness and friendship.

Lastly, I would like to acknowledge those who have not only influenced me but who have taken so much personal time to help teach me and train me in the word of God. Dr. James White, John Lalgee, Scott Goodwill, Randy Rhea, Randall Littleton, my mom who introduced me to the Bible, my brother Patrick, Steve Noblett, Rick Miller, Mylon Lefevre. In all gratefulness and humility I want to thank you. It has been life changing. All that we have been given is of grace, and all that is made is for His glory. Thank you.

NOTES

[1] Matthew Henry, *Matthew Henry's Commentary on the Whole Bible: New Modern Edition* (1991; repr., Peabody, MA: Hendrickson Publishers Marketing, LLC, 2017), 5:79.

[2] Henry, *Matthew Henry's Commentary on the Whole Bible*, 5:79.

[3] Skillet, "Stars," 2016, Track 3 on *Unleashed*, Atlantic Records, 2016, compact disc.

[4] Brian Duigan, "Postmodernism," Britannica.com, September 4, 2020, https://www.britannica.com/topic/postmodernism-philosophy.

[5] "Relativism," Oxfordreference.com, https://www.oxfordreference.com/view/10.1093/oi/authority.20110803100412717.

[6] Maria Baghramian and J. Adam Carter, "Relativism," *Stanford Encyclopedia of Philosophy*, Plato.Stanford.edu, September 15, 2020, https://plato.stanford.edu/entries/relativism/.

[7] Brian Duigan, "Postmodernism," Britannica.com, September 4, 2020, https://www.britannica.com/topic/postmodernism-philosophy.

[8] Jordan Peterson, "Postmodernism: Definition and Critique (with a Few Comments on Its Relationship with Marxism)," JordanPeterson.com, https://www.jordanbpeterson.com/philosophy/postmodernism-definition-and-critique-with-a-few-comments-on-its-relationship-with-marxism/.

[9] John Frame, *The Doctrine of God* (Phillipsburg, NJ: P&R Publishing Company, 2002), 475.

[10] John Frame, *The Doctrine of the Word of God* (Phillipsburg, NJ: P&R Publishing Company, 2010), 50.

[11] John Frame, *The Doctrine of the Word of God* (Phillipsburg, NJ: P&R Publishing Company, 2010), 88.

[12] Louis Berkhof, *Berkhof's Systematic Theology*, rev. ed. (1949; repr., Ingersoll, Canada: Devoted Publishing, 2019), 165.

[13] Louis Berkhof, *Berkhof's Systematic Theology*, rev. ed. (1949; repr., Ingersoll, Canada: Devoted Publishing, 2019), 174.

[14] Matthew Henry, *Matthew Henry's Commentary on the Whole Bible: New Modern Edition* (1991; repr., Peabody, MA: Hendrickson Publishers Marketing, LLC, 2017), 5:20.

[15] Louis Berkhof, *Berkhof's Systematic Theology*, rev. ed. (1949; repr., Ingersoll, Canada: Devoted Publishing, 2019), 166.

[16] John Calvin, *Institutes of the Christian Religion* (1536; repr., Peabody, MA: Hendrickson Publishers Marketing, LLC, 2019), 152.

[17] Louis Berkhof, *Berkhof's Systematic Theology*, rev. ed. (1949; repr., Ingersoll, Canada: Devoted Publishing, 2019), 175.

[18] Charles Hodge, *Systematic Theology* (1871; repr., Peabody, MA: Hendrickson Publishers Marketing, LLC, 2016), 1:102.

[19] Charles Hodge, *Systematic Theology* (1871; repr., Peabody, MA: Hendrickson Publishers Marketing, LLC, 2016), 1:103.

[20] Kim Parker and Renee Stepler, "As U.S. Marriage Rate Hovers at 50%, Education Gap in Marital Status Widens," *FactTank: News in the Numbers, Pew Research Center*, Pewresearch.org, September 14, 2017, https://www.pewresearch.org/fact-tank/2017/09/14/as-u-s-marriage-rate-hovers-at-50-education-gap-in-marital-status-widens/.

[21] Gaby Galvin, "U.S. Marriage Rate Hits Historic Low," *U.S. News & World Report*, USnews.com, April 29, 2020, https://www.usnews.com/news/healthiest-communities/articles/2020-04-29/us-marriage-rate-drops-to-record-low.

[22] "Gender, Family and Marriage, Same-Sex Marriage and Religion," *Pew Research Center: U.S. Politics and Policy*, Pewresearch.org, December 17, 2019, https://www.pewresearch.org/politics/2019/12/17/5-gender-family-and-marriage-same-sex-marriage-and-religion/.

[23] Meghan Holohan, "Birth rates in the US decline to lowest level in 35 years," Today.com, May 20, 2020, https://www.today.com/health/2019-birth-rates-birth-rates-us-decline-lowest-level-35-t182033.

[24] A. Pawlowski, "Why aren't millennials having kids? 8 insights into the child-free life," Today.com, June 10, 2019, https://www.today.com/health/why-aren-t-millennials-having-kids-8-insights-child-free-t155804.

[25] Claire Cain Miller, "Americans Are Having Fewer Babies. They Told Us Why." *The New York Times*, NYtimes.com, July 5, 2018, https://www.nytimes.com/2018/07/05/upshot/americans-are-having-fewer-babies-they-told-us-why.html.

[26] Nattavudh Powdthavee, "Think having children will make you happy?" *The British Psychologist Society*, thepsychologist.bps.org.uk, April 2009, https://thepsychologist.bps.org.uk/volume-22/edition-4/think-having-children-will-make-you-happy.

[27] Hannah Miller, "US suicide rate rises 40% over 17 years, with blue-collar workers at highest risk, CDC finds," CNBC.com, January 23, 2020, https://www.cnbc.com/2020/01/23/us-suicide-rates-rise-40percent-over-17-years-with-blue-collar-workers-at-highest-risk-cdc-finds.html.

[28] "The State of Mental Health in America," *Mental Health America*, Mhanational.org, https://www.mhanational.org/issues/state-mental-health-america.

[29] Katherine Kam, "Mental Health an Emerging Crisis of COVID Pandemic," *WebMD*, Webmd.com, May 8, 2020, https://www.webmd.com/lung/news/20200508/mental-health-emerging-crisis-of-covid-pandemic.

[30] Amanda Jackson, "A crisis mental-health hotline has seen an 891% spike in calls," CNN.com, April 10, 2020, https://www.cnn.com/2020/04/10/us/disaster-hotline-call-increase-wellness-trnd/index.html.

[31] A. W. Tozer, *The Knowledge of the Holy* (New York, NY: HarperCollins Publishers, 1961), 97.

[32] John Frame, *The Doctrine of God* (Phillipsburg, NJ: P&R Publishing Company, 2002), 463.

[33] John Frame, *The Doctrine of God* (Phillipsburg, NJ: P&R Publishing Company, 2002), 467.

[34] John Frame, *The Doctrine of God* (Phillipsburg, NJ: P&R Publishing Company, 2002), 458.

[35] John Piper, "What is Idolatry?" *Ask Pastor John, desiringGod*, desiringgod.org, August 19, 2014, https://www.desiringgod.org/interviews/what-is-idolatry.

[36] Charles Hodge, *Systematic Theology* (1871; repr., Peabody, MA: Hendrickson Publishers Marketing, LLC, 2016), 1:101.

[37] Scotty Smith, *Objects of His Affection: Coming Alive to the Compelling Love of God* (West Monroe: Howard Publishing Co., Inc., 2001), 6.

[38] John Piper, "The Covenant of Abraham," *desiringGod*, desiringgod.org, October 18, 1981, https://www.desiringgod.org/messages/the-covenant-of-abraham.

[39] "Ellicott's Commentary for English Readers," 2 Corinthians 5, Studylight.org, https://www.studylight.org/commentaries/ebc/2-corinthians-5.html.

All scripture quotations unless otherwise noted are from the ESV® Bible (The Holy Bible, English Standard Version®), copyright © 2001 by Crossway, a publishing ministry of Good News Publishers. Used by permission. All rights reserved.